Stories Previously Published

"The Demo Flight" ["Buckets and Buttons"]
– Vertical Magazine - Aug/Sep 2010

"The Most Gorgeous Thing, Ever"
– *Aviation International News* - March 2011

"Plan 'B' from Deepest Arizona" ["Okay, Plan B It Is!"]
– Vertical Magazine - Apr/May 2011

"Tackling the Cessna 140"
– Vertical *Online* - Apr 2011

"Pilot in a Painter's Paradox" ["A Brush with Fate"]
– Vertical Magazine - Jun/Jul 2012

"Exorcising the Evil Aircraft"
– Vertical Magazine - Feb/Mar 2013

CAPTAIN METHANE
and his Finely Feathered Friends

"The Mark Twain of Helicopter Pilots?"

by
DORCEY ALAN WINGO

Author of
Wind Loggers &
The Rise and Fall of Captain Methane

Captain Methane and his Finely Feathered Friends
Copyright © 2021 by Dorcey Alan Wingo

All rights reserved. No part of this publication may be reproduced, distributed, or transmitted in any form or by any means, including photocopying, recording, or other electronic or mechanical methods, without the prior written permission of the author, except in the case of brief quotations embodied in critical reviews and certain other non-commercial uses permitted by copyright law.

ISBN
978-1-956161-43-4 (Paperback)
978-1-956161-42-7 (eBook)

Credits for Photos and Illustrations

Illustrator Chris Rohrmoser: Custom illustrations for the following original stories:

The Demo Flight, Plan "B" From Deeper Arizona, Pilot in a Painter's Paradox, and *Exorcising the Evil Aircraft.*

Photo of the Author by Lourdes M. Wingo.
All other photographs by the Author.

TABLE OF CONTENTS

Foreword ix

The Most Gorgeous Thing, Ever 1
Who Knows the Crow? 5
Blanche Beulah's Purple Pinworm Paranoia 10
Pendejo on the Comm Center Floor 15
Kung Fu Skip 24
Denny and the Key 28
Plan "B" from Deeper Arizona 35
The Captain in Grass Pants 40
The Demo Flight 44
182 to Red Bluff 49
There Will be Blood! 53
Tackling the Cessna 140 57
The Secret Protocol of Cul-de-Sac Spring 61
Have Lama, Will Trailer 65
The Big Shipment 69
Pilot in a Painter's Paradox 72
The One-Handed Mechanic 77
Flight of the Engineer 80
Static Electricity and Going Fetal 83
Handles 86

Babbling Bob and the Black Hole 89
Exorcising the Evil Aircraft 91
Trojan Moonbus 95
CW2 Gregory George Beck 100
The Animal... 108
Captain Michael P. "Mic" O'connor...121
William T. Dvorak.. 129

Mama Celia's Culíche Style Chicken Móle....................................... 144
Glossary 146

FOREWORD

By Elan Head

I first heard the name Dorcey Wingo from Tony Fonze, the editor of *Autorotate Magazine*. It was early in my flying career, and I was still wrapping my mind around the helicopter industry: still learning about the incredible variety of uses to which helicopters could be put, and the unique subcultures associated with each. Tony described Dorcey as "the Mark Twain of the helicopter industry" — a description that made an impression on me then, and has stuck with me ever since. Somehow I knew instantly that, by it, Tony meant not only a gifted storyteller with a keen ear for dialogue and eye for detail, but also a humorist who could illuminate the helicopter industry's subcultures with sympathy and insight.

As the years went by, and I became first a reader, then an editor of Dorcey's work, I came to appreciate those qualities more and more. Those of us in the helicopter industry love what we do with a passion: we love helicopters and flying, and we love to talk about them. But I've seen enough significant others' eyes glaze over in cocktail-party conversation to know that very few pilots are good at communicating that passion to people outside of the industry. Stories that to us are laced with adrenaline and meaning become dull and tedious when told in mixed company. Dorcey is one of the few pilots who *can* translate helicopter stories for a wider audience, picking up on those human details that resonate with everyone, even people who have never touched a "cyclic." Outsiders may never completely understand why helicopter pilots make the sacrifices we do, but they'll come a lot closer to grasping it after reading Captain Methane.

During the time I spent as editor-in-chief of *Vertical* Magazine, I edited a number of the stories included in this volume as "There I Was" columns for the magazine. "There I Was" columns are exactly what the name suggests — first-person accounts of moments that were particularly harrowing or humbling — and Dorcey has as many of those as anyone in the industry. Appearing here in their full glory, with none of the regrettable editing that was demanded by space constraints in the magazine, these stories showcase Dorcey's terrific knack for spinning a yarn. So do the many stories that, for one reason or another, didn't make it into our trade magazine — I have a particular fondness for "Who Knows the Crow," in which Captain Methane applies his descriptive powers to finely feathered friends of the literal kind.

Captain Methane has so many exploits to his credit that, on the page, he can come across as larger than life. But Dorcey's friends know that he's also a deeply kind and thoughtful person who, in addition to humor, brings a great deal of reflection to his writing. In this book, he's also proven himself to be a conscientious reporter, dedicated to sharing incredible stories besides his own. Which brings me to the story in this volume that I find most remarkable: the story of Captain William T. Dvorak. It's an extraordinary tale, well told — a contribution not only to the helicopter industry's historical record, but also to literature in general.

Whether he's writing about himself or others, Dorcey's stories are invariably grounded in sharp observation and rich experience. Not that you'd expect anything else from the helicopter industry's Samuel Clemens. Mark Twain himself observed that "experience is an author's most valuable asset; experience is the thing that puts the muscle and the breath and the warm blood into the book he writes." Breathing life into the page is what Dorcey does best, which is why it has been an honor for me to read and edit his work and, now, to introduce it. Thank you, Captain!

THE MOST GORGEOUS THING, EVER

Is not the woman to whom I am married?

Anyone who knows me well can verify that I married a great looking lady; the fairest in all the land, in my eyes. But as pretty as she is, Lourdes is not the loveliest thing I have ever seen. That special feast-for-eyeballs came about during my very last Huey flight in the U.S. Army.

Lessons learned in Army Aviation should include this warning: If you are the unit's "short timer" pilot, don't be surprised near the end of the day when the head honcho hands you the logbook to a tired old helicopter, and he's got a peculiar look on his face.

Like me, you may soon be off on a cross-country flight in a bird that is too problematical to perform routine missions. It sounds reassuring to hear the Operations Chief say, "You can probably make it all the way to Stockton (Army Depot - "The Repo Depo") before something really bad happens."

One peek in the troubled logbook tells the story: more than half of the gripes are signed-off as "Circle Red-X" conditions. That means the repairs needed on the bird exceed the maintenance capabilities of the home unit, and the helicopter must be ferried to the Repo Depo in Central California for field maintenance. (At least the avionics work!)

Walking out to the Holloman AFB ramp early the next morning, I took in the somber-looking, olive-drab Army UH-1H sitting near the taxi-way. The young Army rotorcraft mechanic, accompanying me on the cross-country (XC) flight to Stockton, was adding engine oil to the reservoir and buttoning up the air-intake screens; almost ready to depart.

This was my first "solo" XC in what was normally a dual-piloted Army slick. It was thus a rare treat for "Lucky" - my Crew Chief who normally flies in the back, latched onto an armed M-60 machine gun in wartime - or keeping an eye out for passengers who don't listen to his safety briefings.

Lucky came from parts unknown, but he was clearly happy to be riding in the left front seat for a change. Now he'd be getting some stick time from a veteran CW2 and enjoying the up-front-Cadillac-wide-screen version of the legendary Huey.

We traveled light and planned to make the fifteen-hundred-mile flight in a couple days, the old bird willing. Back in two days - with a little travel pay – *that's* the Army way.

Holloman Tower bid us adieu in the long shadows of dawn. We lit off westbound, with clearance to cross the Restricted Area, low level. The battered old bird rumbled along into a mild headwind, indicating 100 knots - and not the smoothest flying Iroquois I've ever strapped on.

Cruising west at a thousand feet abeam White Sands National Monument, we were rocked moderately crossing over the dramatic "pipes" of the Organ Mountains. Passing by Las Cruces Municipal Airport, we clattered our way over the high mesa to Deming, our first fuel point. Lucky was showing promise as a *stick*, I recall, but there was nothing else very memorable on that desert XC flight, all the way across Arizona and on to Palm Springs. And then......it got memorable.

Our long, slow approach down into the L.A. Basin toward Ontario Airport - following the railroad on our sectional map - was complicated by an increasingly thick haze of smog.

It was actually purple on the horizon ahead of us, and the ambient odor was acrid. Tall smokestacks belched more of the same from a stark, gray steel mill. Acres of wrecked automobiles in massive bone-yards, and miles of congested rail yards passed by our plastic windows. It was an apprehensive leg, through some of the worst smog[1] I have ever navigated.

Dialing in the Ontario Tower, we were relieved to hear a friendly voice. The Fed steered us his way during a lull in airliner traffic. We followed his vectors and soon observed the tire-scarred numbers "26" pass under our chin bubbles. We hover-taxied over to the Jet-A service helipad, located near the base of the [old] FAA Tower. The smog burned our eyes! We managed to get some encouraging info from the weather people as our Huey was refueled and we grabbed a light snack. Afterward, Lucky had

---

[1] This flight occurred in the spring of 1971: LA smog at its worst!

ample opportunity to add more oil to our leaky Lycoming. Our destination (Stockton) was reported to be VFR with a broken ceiling, winds light and variable. Preflight looks good, other than an oily engine deck. Now to carve our way out of this purple haze and head for Yosemite National Park!

Got an okay from the Tower to climb on course through the crud to VFR-on-top, which we did regularly in the military (single engine) with never a glitch. Breaking out around six thousand feet, the dazzling white cloud tops were wonderful to behold, and the carbon-and-sulfur stench was gone. Requesting cruise speed from my left-seater, I studied the map against the terrain below. Lucky's magnetic heading appeared to parallel the pencil line on our colorful map.

Looking things over, we had plenty of fuel, and lots of breaks in the clouds. Our path was on course, and steady as she goes. I made our position reports with Flight Watch on time, and then, as we climbed ever so gradually to clear the fluffy cloud tops ahead, we passed the midway point of our fuel load and *something* electrical in the old ship simply died.

Something that would disable our radios, nav-instruments, and our transponder, with nary a voltmeter glitch or master caution light. There was no electrical odor. We both looked for solutions but quickly discovered that the problem was not circuit-breaker-related, and fortunately - did not affect her dependable turbine engine.

About the time we whirled past cloud-obscured Yosemite, I began to get really nervous. Breaks in the clouds were getting fewer and farther between. Navigating became a case of over-the-top, time, distance and heading. Higher we climbed, closing the air vents as cold air whistled in.

Lucky didn't begin to tell me what to do; this was my problem, and he was along for the ride. When I calculated that we were nearing the Stockton vicinity, I feared messing with airline traffic. And if we flew too far west, we'd be over the Pacific.

Our fuel dropped to a measly 200 pounds, assuming that the gauge was correct. With no breaks in the clouds, fear was welling up in my gut as I made large circles and dialed the emergency code into the transponder, praying it would alert the regional radar facility. But the radios were dead. They appeared to be on, but there was no audible "squelch" and no reply light on the transponder. Ten thousand feet and running out of ideas.

At one hundred pounds indicated, I realized I must begin an instrument descent and rely on pure luck to get us through the thick mass before our ten minutes of fuel was burned up. Dreading this last ditch maneuver more than anything, I began to slow the big helicopter down and lowered the power. The raw fear that had been boiling within me suddenly began a one-way rumbling advance in my gut and my priorities were quickly reversed!

I sat frozen in the right seat, glancing over at Lucky to see if he was "as afraid" as I was.

He was transfixed, staring at the fuel gauge: this was a first for him, too.

So that old expression of being "...so scared he crapped his pants!" wasn't just an expression, it dawned on me!

About the time I bottomed the collective pitch to descend blindly into the deep sea of clouds, I saw *the most gorgeous thing* on planet Earth: a coral-blue opening appeared immediately off to starboard, a thirty-foot wide "sucker-hole," sent by Heavenly Express! An incredibly beautiful green pasture beckoned, nine thousand feet directly below us, if I could just dive right in there and stay visually oriented inside the now greenish-blue vertical tunnel, all the way down.

Dialing back the turbine-engine-trim for a rapid descent to the right, that irresistible impulse in my bowels quickly subsided and the "yee-haws" from Lucky told me he was feeling much better about our prospects. Spiraling all the way down with our tail section in the white stuff, the sucker hole stayed open, and we broke out at about 500 feet above the ground, plenty of time to beep-up the engine speed and take a deep breath!

The lush green meadow became our LZ, conveniently bordered on the east by a full-service gas station where we used the pay phone to call the Repo Depo. We could actually see the facility from the meadow! The Depot pilots were old hands at this sort of thing and told us, "Leave 'er there, boys. We'll come get 'er."

Ha! They didn't have to twist our arms. And I honestly don't remember my mechanic's name after so many years; but after that flight, he was "Lucky" to me!

WHO KNOWS THE CROW?

My first exposure to *Corvus corax* – the raven or common crow - was as a youth in Sundown, Texas. An upper classman had a "pet" crow that used to fly to school with him on occasion. Meanest damned bird I ever saw. He'd either ride along on the kid's shoulder or fly menacing circles around him, just overhead. The sleek black critter would **CAW** his head off, too - frilling his neck feathers out like bristles on a bottle brush.

At inopportune times, the crow would drop down on the least suspecting of many children gathered on the grassy school playground. Landing on a screaming young girl's head I recall - talons extended – while cawing loudly and flapping its broad black wings. It was a scene right out of Hitchcock's, *The Birds*. But this was years before the movie, and this was nonfiction.

The "upper classman" had no more control over his "pet" than anyone else, so it was bad news when either he or the crow showed up. There was a growing list of citizenry from Sundown who had been pecked, scratched - or *dumped on* - by the big bad bird. The crow never attacked lucky ol' me, but I was wary of him, nonetheless. Turns out, I had a lot to learn about crows.

In Native American Indian lore, the raven has special significance. You'll probably never see an authentic totem pole – one hand-carved by a northwestern American Native - that is ***not*** topped by a raven. The northwestern Indians consider *Corvus corax* to be a sacred bird. It's bad juju to top a totem pole with anything else. (That may explain why one never sees a totem *pole* with a pole *cat* on top.)

o o o o o

Many years later while working as a jungle pilot in Peru, I had ample free time to study my feathered friends around camp. Easiest to observe were the *Cathartes aura*; the local black and white "turkey buzzard." They are more often than not referred to as *zopilotes* in South America.

As the lush green jungle heats up in the sweltering sun, currents of warm, moist air rise high into the heavens. Zopilotes by the hundreds flutter from local tree tops and take flight. Gliding effortlessly upward on Nature's invisible elevator for a lofty view from the cool air above, the cumulus-carpeted sky is soon spackled with swirling gyres of black and white buzzards.

Circling lazily clockwise and counterclockwise, one formation stacks above another and before long, hundreds of soaring vultures participate in a feathery air show. Whenever they got tired or spotted some "fresh" carrion below, they began to descend individually from way up yonder in a screaming dive that was not only visible, it could also be heard.

When one of these buzzards decided it was time to return to the jungle, he simply folded up his wings, extended his neck, and plummeted earthward like a streamlined wall-safe.

If the casual observer is within a hundred meters or so, he can easily hear the *Stuka dive bomber* sound a turkey vulture's feathers make toward the end of its dive - at terminal velocity - their leathery red "helmets" flapping away like cartoon characters.

Other zopilotes soon followed the lead, dropping randomly from the sky until the clouds were all alone - and the weary tree tops were heavily draped in sulking, hungry buzzards.

o o o o o

The intelligence of a crow is considered to be superior to most other birds, and is perhaps on the level of the wily coyote. I have a hard time trying to explain the bizarre behavior I observed driving into the school district's office once, where my wife worked.

A small family of crows had settled on the deep green lawn next to the Administration Building, where a discarded paper lunch sack had tumbled out of a waste container. The crows were busily handing out all the goodies they discovered in the paper bag, including one of those clear "disposable" plastic drinking cups.

To the young crow closest to me, the cup was way too much fun. He held the intriguing item firmly in his right claw, pinning it to the ground. As I drove slowly by, the crow repeatedly pecked at the thing. But each thrust of his sharp beak was parried by the sturdy slick vessel, shoving his beak obliquely to one side or the other. Again and again he stabbed with the same results. It looked as if he wasn't going to get the message any time soon. I drove on by, shaking my head and laughing to myself about the funny "bird brains!"

o o o o o

Heading north one snowy January morning to return to my loggin' job in Montana, I took off out of Bishop, northeast-bound on my favorite highway. Just inside the Nevada state line, my trusty little Buick purred steadily over Montgomery Pass, a lofty 7,167 feet in elevation.

Slowing to take a familiar pullout ahead, my eye caught the movement of two small black figures gliding along atop a tall snowdrift. Not wanting to scare the playful ravens off, I pulled to a stop early and powered down my windows for an unobstructed view.

I'd heard of ravens playing and rolling in the snow. I even verified that behavior via a nature video I located on the Internet. But what I was observing this sunny day were two black birds lying on their backs, wings folded, and gliding along on their glossy backsides.

The birds simply shoved one leg at a time to propel themselves along on the powdery snow. Staring up at the dark blue sky, they chuckled softly with each other in obvious glee. My camera was beyond reach, and the moment was lost the next instant in a tempest of wind. After a brief blizzard, there was neither sight nor sound to be heard, save the wind whistling through the pines around me. I shook my head in giddy wonder this time, and motored on down the long, blue road.

The following winter my logging crew was working near Seeley Lake, Montana. Every morning I drove north out of "Looney's," a lonely loggers' motel-café - in the middle of nowhere. Motoring north on Highway 83 toward my chopper's Service Landing, I invariably passed the corpses of deer, struck dead by passing motorists; like frozen hamburger alongside the road.

It had been a cold winter and there were numerous deer cadavers lying adjacent to the asphalt. Snowplows had piled three-foot-high drifts along the roadway, and many of the deer bodies were around, the deer lying on top of the snow, exposed to the elements. As the snow melted from corpses, one would pass deer after mangled deer, suspended three feet in in the air on hourglass-shaped pillars of dirty snow.

As the weather warmed, ravens and other birds would flock to the feast, pecking upon what was thawed out. Eventually the corpses would be picked clean of meat or clobbered by a passing snowplow - sending carrion, distracted birds, and bloody bones flying off into the ditch. One crusty old deer had come to rest close to the narrow road's fog line. A couple of crows were sitting atop the remains, pecking away like crazy on the rancid venison. As I rolled slowly by, I could see a third raven had penetrated down inside the deer's rib cage. It was darting around in the *prime rib* that had long been frozen and out of reach. He had fallen to his final feast, trapped by the meaty ribs about him; and his brothers and sisters were panicky.

A mesmerizing encounter with a crow in the road followed within a year or so. Fall was in full bloom in the panhandle of Idaho and I was making my way from St. Maries to St. Regis along the St. Joe River Road. The narrow paved route climbs fairly steeply nearing the Montana state line, with many switch backs to take at slow speed. Golden leaves billowed in crazy clouds as my ride swept by, a stiff breeze blowing at my rear bumper. As I slowed to take the next hairpin to the right, I could scarcely believe what my eyes were feeding to my brain. What was left of an adult crow's body was long mashed hard into the dry pavement. The only recognizable things about the wretched raven were its dusty black wings, which were steadfastly floundering in the up-canyon wind. They were flapping at first in perfect unison, swirling wildly in the gale, and eventually going totally out of sync with each other.

Swerving left to avoid crushing the crow's macabre wingspan, the feathery folly passed beneath my butt and reappeared in my rearview mirrors. Swaying in my vehicle's turbulence, the weird wings resumed their tandem, eerie *flight of the dead,* as I rolled slowly over the rise and into Western Montana. Whenever my thoughts return to those haunting wings of the *Overrun Raven*, my Okie brain never fails to dial up Lenny Kravitz: the familiar *"I want to fly away"* melody.

"Yea, yea, yea!"

∘ ∘ ∘ ∘ ∘

A casual observer of Nature such as I can learn a lot about these mysterious feathery creatures, and never read a published word on the subject. Growing old has its advantages; many things become clearer. Our purpose on this earth might be explained in life's simmering soup, if only we take time to study the amazing ingredients.

Which brings us, fellow bird lovers, to THE creature that gets my personal vote as One Who Knows Crows, and has no problem whatsoever in eating little baby crows left unattended in their nest. Such things go unseen around my SoCal home throughout the early days of summer, but by chance I observed Rialto's local Red Tailed Hawk, trying to evade two pissed off crows.

The ravens were very vocal in their pursuit of the large male *Buteo jamaicensis*, making the big bird climb, dive and twist around half-inverted in flight; parrying their dangerous dives with skillful flying and razor sharp talons. The crows apparently couldn't care less about what the hawk might do to them. They clearly wanted to rip the flying red devil to shreds - as it might have done to their babies. On and on the aerial battle went. I wondered where these creatures stored all the energy needed to fly so hard and fast, and on such a hot day. Right when it looked like the hawk would start taking a beating, he turned straight into the wind and began to climb skyward on reserve energy.

The crows by then were - as they say in baseball - "leaking oil," but the question was, "did they have enough fight left in them to slay the *chicken hawk?*" Three, four, five mighty strokes of his splendid red wings, and the resilient raptor pulled ahead. He was slightly above and in front of the shrieking crows - precisely where he wanted them. The crow closest to the Buteo's black-water trapdoor didn't have a chance. As it flew into the sudden deluge of hawk waste byproducts; the poor crow reeled like it had been hit by a Sidewinder. The crow in trail formation also appeared to have taken a lot of crap. Both of the humiliated birds flew away abruptly toward the southeast, in a silent power dive. They headed no doubt for a cool birdbath with clean towels – far away from Shitty Hawk.

BLANCHE BEULAH'S PURPLE PINWORM PARANOIA

Mom cures me from going fishing.

When I reached the tender young age of ten, Mom and Dad got it into their heads to go "fishin'" again. Never mind that we almost got trampled in a cattle stampede on our previous outing at Possum Kingdom Lake. Dad learned not to pitch the tent near a salt lick on that near-death episode. But me being the low man on the totem pole, I knew better than to protest. I was goin' and that was that.

When the day arrived for us to start packing to leave, my heavily bespectacled Mom emerged from the ladies' room in a huff. She announced to all within earshot that she had seen "evidence of a pinworm." Once "Blanche" gets an idea like that in her Oklahoma head, all the certified *wormologists* in Texas could not convince her otherwise. Pinworms[2], I wondered?

To save us from such a terrible fate and further complicate our travels, Mom began administering a regimen of small purple, over-the-counter pills for what "we" had. Dad threw up his hands, blew off some steam, took his purple poison, and resumed packing.

Part of the motivation for this trip was the new one-wheeled camper-trailer Dad had built at the local high school. He taught the woodworking course there - with a little World History on the side - but working with wood was definitely J.B. Wingo's thing.

Our teardrop-shaped camper-trailer began life as a mail-order kit, which came with a rudimentary steel and aluminum frame. Its primary cost-saving feature was the solitary swiveling, spring-loaded wheel with a rubber tire - like those found on the common wheelbarrow. Dad built the

---

[2] Enterobius vermicularis – the most common intestinal parasite in the US.

trailer during the second semester with help from his woodshop students. Our fishing trip to Washita[3] was to be its virgin voyage.

The camper rig bolted to the rear frame of our 1956 Plymouth Savoy by way of two beefy steel arms, which also kept the rig level. There was a "catch," of course. We learned as soon as we backed into our camping space above the dam in Arkansas that our one-wheeled wonder's swiveling tire could lock sideways in the process of backing up.

Dad didn't see the problem in his tiny mirror. When the trailer stopped suddenly and rose slightly, he mashed down harder on the gas, impatient to park and get all the backseat drivers and noisy kids out of his hair. And ***eeerrrrrk***, just like that - the trailer's beefy attachment arms bent like butter under the torque of the Plymouth's growling V-8.

Now J.B. was fit to be tied. Digging out his "emergency tools" from the trunk, the damaged trailer had to be unbolted, jacked around manually and blocked up solid before we could free-up our car, much less remove the distorted trailer arms for repair. We guys also had to pitch the heavy six-man canvas tent and get the girls going on some grub.

To seal my fate, my sister Joy and I had attracted scores of menacing little red mites known as "chiggers" while playing outside the Old House in Springer, the previous day. You just couldn't contain a couple of city kids with domesticated farm animals around and tall grass in the fields. The chiggers hopped on us before we even thought about 'em, and we were both itching in our undies by suppertime. And right on time, Blanche was there to hand out them purple pills of hers.

We finally got the tent up the next evening, all the air mattresses pumped up firm; close to turning the gas lantern off for the night. That was when my sister asked Mom what she might have in her bag of tricks for itchy chigger bites. Blanche replied that the Okie treatment for chiggers was to pour a little kerosene on a rag and rub the affected area with it. It is supposed to kill the chiggers overnight. Kind of smelly, though.

Naturally, Dad had a can of just about everything in the camper-trailer, so both my sister and I applied a small measure of kerosene on a rag to rid ourselves of the nasty little critters. According to legend, they'd check out as we slept, while Mom's purple pinworm pills were doing their work.

---

[3] Lake Ouachita is in west central Arkansas. We had a lot of fun with the name, too.

When the brilliant sun broke through the tall trees the next morning, Dad and my brother Jon were already getting the campfire going and boiling up some coffee in the big black percolator over our three-burner Coleman stove. Mom was right behind them, eager to get breakfast going and start fishing. Joy showed some spunk and poured a glass of OJ while I lay in the sleeping bag and took a long look between my legs in an effort to comprehend what the corrosive kerosene had done to my crotch.

I wasn't listening if anyone said anything about removing one's underwear after anointing one's inner thighs and groin with kerosene, so the fumes don't last all night and burn the skin. The worst part of my ordeal was yet to come, but simply having to bare myself while Mom inspected my boyhood and those crude red rashes around it was a major blow to my dignity.

Mom wasted no time in declaring me a bed-case. "You can't go anywhere or wear any clothing until that rash goes down," she explained, handing me a paper plate heaped with bacon and scrambled eggs. *"Meaning what,"* I asked? "You can hang out here in the tent while we're gone fishing. There's food in the pantry. We won't be gone long. You'll be fine." In other words, Mom was goin' fishin' and a little diaper rash wasn't going to stop her. Man, that was precisely what I needed to hear, because I sure didn't want to go anywhere in the condition I was in. Mom followed up breakfast with another purple pill, the last one in the series, she told us proudly, and I suddenly had something to be happy about. Pretty soon the fishing poles were loaded in the Plymouth, and I waved "adios" from the privacy of our cozy tent, with a towel wrapped around my middle.

Things were pretty neat around the campground for about an hour, and then all those purple pills I'd been poppin' hit me at once. It suddenly dawned on me that I hadn't made a serious stop at any of the little boys' rooms since we left our hometown over two days before. Panic set in when I realized the nearest appliance was in the bathhouse, 200 feet down the forested path.

Grabbing a beltless pair of Levis, I slid into both legs as quickly as possible, leaving some room at the crotch for my wicked diaper rash. Feeling a rumble in my innards, I anticipated that there was no time for lacing up sneakers, nor even socks for that matter. It was out-the-tent-flap and down the path I went, saying over and over to myself, "I'm going to make it! I'm going to make it! I'm going to make it!!"Meanwhile, down in the spiffy bathhouse, two teenaged boys had just finished taking a refreshing dip in the river and are laughing and joking as they towel-off near the showers.

Who else but *Purple Pinworm Boy* comes sloshing up through the open doorway - bow-legged - clutching the top halves of his unbuttoned blue jeans in either hand. Trailing along behind him are two purple streams, flowing out of his trouser legs and following him around the corner. *Pinworm Boy* briefly stands in the open doorway, casting a long shadow in their direction. The teenagers fell silent. Avoiding eye-to-eye contact, I made straight for the nearest appliance, freeing up one hand long enough to push the stall's wooden door open, slither inside, and lock the door. With no further introduction, I tuned out the teenagers and made up for lost time. My bathhouse guests left right after that, whispering as they tippy-toed outside.

Once I was satisfied that I could carry on again, I rounded up my terrible trousers and made to leave, status quo. This was an old-fangled toilet, but finally I found the flush-handle suspended by a chain from the high-mounted water tank and gave 'er a mighty flush or two.

Trousers in tow, I let myself out of the stall and moved straight into the shower, making as few tracks as possible, and hosing myself and my jeans down like I did this kind of stuff every day. Incredibly, no one walked in while I was showering myself off!

Being careful where I stepped, I made my way out the door and stole back up toward the tent, wearing only my soaking wet blue jeans. I took a different route this time; *the purple trail* would go unused during the rest of our stay. Back at the tent I was feeling more like my old self. I wrapped my bod in a towel, hung my jeans out to dry near the campfire and made like everything was hunky-dory.

An hour or so before the fishing party returned to check on me, I watched from on high as the familiar green Campground Service pickup truck pulled off the highway and made its way toward the bathhouse. I could distinctly hear the male driver whistling a cheery Walt Disney tune[4] as he parked near the entrance and walked methodically toward the men's room with a couple of fresh rolls of TP.

---

4   "Zip-a-dee-do-dah, zip-a-dee-ay…"

As the happy host disappeared from view, his cheerful whistle died. The same man - less all the enthusiasm - returned slowly to his truck, head down and hushed. I watched with complete understanding as he set the twin rolls of TP back where they came from and made for a battered snow shovel, stashed vertically in the bed of his truck. Back he headed into the bathhouse - shovel in hand - looking tired and repulsed.

To this day, I can't remember if we caught any fish on that trip, because once the fishermen returned to camp and I told 'em my *purple pinworm* story, it became the highlight of the whole vacation. Mom put away her bag of tricks after that, and was I ever relieved!

PENDEJO ON THE COMM CENTER FLOOR

Overnight Military Career Changers

President Johnson's spit had dried little more than ten months on the envelope of my 1966 Draft Notice by the time *yours truly* found himself 10,000 miles away in Bangkok, Thailand. The Private First Class version of me descending from the Boeing 707 was a freshly trained Army 72B20, *Communications Center Specialist*. This was the job I *thought* I'd be content with until my helicopter flight school application was approved, as the Vietnam "conflict" ground on.

"Comm Centers," as they are known, handle virtually all important communications in the military theater. Military types who cater to work in this environment get their quota of top secret messages and high tech, top secret machinery - once they gain access to the high security, air-conditioned chambers.

A novice 72B20 can type at least 35 words per minute (WPM) on a standard military keyboard. That kind of "speed" will keep him working on the Comm Center floor. However, if the novice can "poke" 60 to 80 WPM, the Officer-In-Charge (OIC) will park his talented butt in a chair and he will be required to grind out long tedious code groups for the duration of his overseas tour.

Messages go out either in plain text or worst-case scenario – the dreaded multi-letter code groups. God forbid. The Unit's hardcore 72B**40**s - who were superior in skill to the average 72B**20** - grew mystically addicted to code groups, I was to discover.

A seasoned code puncher would go into something akin to a trance, poking those redundant code groups. Hardly ever would he see a word in plain English. He'd sit for hours poking out the likes of CKRPL BJEBN

AMIYT CGEMQ. The mechanical process of scrambling everything with all the machinery was fascinating; the work itself was hectic.

If traffic allowed, the code puncher could stand up and take a break every couple of hours; go outside and smoke a Pall Mall. Never ever would he talk about what he was working on: *mum's the word*. Stuff the cancer stick into the bucket of sand, drain the ol' radiator; go back inside.

Before he knew it, the code puncher had poked his way through another eight hour shift. The replacements arrived, and he shuffled into the same old hot, smoky bus; headed back to town. The ride back to Quarters was usually at high speed, in the dark, and needlessly dramatic.

Our Thai bus drivers drove like outraged zombies, more often than not. One of our notoriously wired SP5 Comm Center guys shouted obscenities at them when they pumped the gas pedal like an old treadle-powered sewing machine. The drivers never seemed to hear "Dave."

While I admired the abilities and mental detachment of my peers, punching codes truly made my head spin. I didn't relish sitting on my butt all day, and I couldn't poke faster than 35 WPM - so it was *The Floor* for me! A least I could type standing up and stay busy the whole shift.

The only fun I ever had back then was burning all of the classified material toward the end of every shift. This took place in our secure compound's aspirated incinerator. The task was witnessed by an armed Military Policeman, 24/7. The MPs would help toss mounds of paperwork, teletype ribbons and millions of tiny chad into the roaring blast furnace. So it went on.

The whole idea of working in a Comm Center spawned from my youthful interest in intelligence work. This likely came from reading the compelling exploits of British Secret Agent *James Bond* in a number of Ian Fleming's literary thrillers of the time. *Pussy Galore* also caught my interest.

The poster on the Las Cruces, New Mexico Army Recruiter's office window advised: *High School Grads, sign up for helicopter flight training!* An Army Huey dominated the graphics. I had dreamed of flying a helicopter for the longest time. *Yep - that's me -* I said to myself - and went on inside.

A handsome young Army Staff Sergeant met me coming in. He smiled, shaking my nervous nineteen-year-old hand. The recruiter invited me over to his desk, motioning to a nice, comfortable chair. I must have looked preoccupied when I handed him my Draft Notice. He glanced briefly at the postmark on LBJ's familiar one page order. In ten days, the new federal regulation stated, I will automatically be inducted - unless I enlisted beforehand.

I told the recruiter I wanted to fly helicopters. "One problem, though," I said. "I'm somewhat colorblind." The Sergeant's brow bunched up when he heard that news, and he looked me over; smiling less intensely. He glanced again at my Draft Notice: reading between the lines - clearly in thinking mode. His temples pounded. Gears were grinding away inside his closely-cropped, military skull.

In the end, the recruiter wasn't put off by the slightly negative aspect of my application. He spoke slowly and thoughtfully, saying that there *were* vacancies in Army Security. He opened a folder and pointed to the ASA symbol: an eagle clutching lightning bolts in its talons. I would later discover that ASA members were referred to as *Lightning-Fast Chicken F-ers*, (or) perhaps more accurately, *Chairborne!*

"A minimum four year enlistment, though," he stressed. "Assuming you zip right through basic training and stay out of trouble. You must graduate from Signal School and maintain your physical fitness. Last two steps: impress the Officer Review Board and score high on the Flight Selection Test. You're in! Should you drop out of flight school for any reason - without a high priority MOS to fall back on - you'll go straight into the Infantry." He was dead serious.

Vietnam, I flashed. The latest *Life Magazine* I leafed through was filled with graphic color photos of jungle warfare. Muddy G.I.s in bloody bandages, booby-traps and black body bags. I imagined a human tide of angry Viet Cong in black pajamas, charging in my direction with their AK-47s. Not to mention all their captured French automatic rifles, festooned with long, sharp bayonets.

Four years is no big deal, I remember thinking. I loved a challenge. Optimistically speaking, I could just fly *above* all the bad guys, snakes and misery - and everything would be Okie-dokie? Hopefully, them Cong can't shoot straight. I was feelin' lucky. And I had nothing better to do.

"If you want to play it safe," the recruiter advocated, rescuing me from jungle vibes, "...sign up for the ASA and hopefully you can pass a top level security check of your background. While that's soaking in, you should pick a *high priority MOS* from this list."

He placed a glossy brief in my hands. "After your Comm Center training is over and you settle into your first duty assignment, apply for flight school. That way, if your color vision or something else trips you up mid-way, the Agency will reel you back on into the fold. No Infantry duty for you."

MOS stands for "Military Occupational Specialty," and for some reason I pictured the Communications Center as the most interesting place to work. "The air conditioning is for the heat-sensitive machinery," the recruiter admitted with a bit of sarcasm. I liked the part about working in secure, air conditioned compounds. So I signed up fast - like a good little chicken plucker.

Turns out the recruiter was *right on the money* with his consultation. From Basic Training at Fort Leonard Wood, Missouri, to Signal School way down south in Dixie, I was marched around and occasionally injected, educated, inspected, tested, and eventually graduated.

Short-timer draftees I met along the way would see the bold ASA patch on my sleeve and howl like chimpanzees about my **FOUR YEAR OBLIGATION**. The draftees would serve only two years and return to civilian life.

"*FOUR YEARS?!*" the draftees would shriek.

"I'm going to fly choppers," was my standard response, which shut a few of 'em up.

Another argued, "You'll get shot down!"

Oh the joys of being a volunteer in a shark infested sea of malcontents, I thought. It'll be a long four years, either way.

After I arrived at my destination, I discovered that we were headquartered in a [3 star] hotel north of downtown. After a week of orientation, painting many stationary objects military green, and more injections, I began taking the nerve-wracking bus ride to "Unit."

How did I like my new job, you might be asking? Well friends, it took less than a week in the Comm Center for me to conclude that working there could ruin a person's whole day. "I'm going to fly choppers," was my standard response, which shut a few of 'em up. Another argued, "You'll get shot down!" Oh the joys of being a volunteer in a shark infested sea of malcontents, I thought. It'll be a long four years, either way.

After I arrived at my destination, I discovered that we were headquartered in a [3 star] hotel north of downtown. After a week of orientation, painting many stationary objects military green, and more injections, I began taking the nerve-wracking bus ride to "The Unit."

How did I like my new job, you might be asking? Well friends, it took less than a week in the Comm Center for me to conclude ***that*** was ***the place to go*** if one wanted to screw up a perfectly good day.

Having worked among the noisy machines in training, I was all too familiar with the big mess the clanking devices made at one of several different stations; not to mention their oily-hot-odor. The machinery smelled like the old toy electric locomotives of my youth. Comm Center types like me had to work hard to keep up with the traffic. If we got caught up, it was the 72B20s who swept up buckets of litter from over under, in and around the messy contraptions.

Unlike the slower machines that we trained on, the Comm Center's machines were set to operate at max-designed speed, which back then was 100 WPM. Until something **broke**, and then the complicated myriad of darting steel fingers and springs would either quit outright or break down with great fanfare; like a thoroughbred horse with a busted leg.

Whenever a breakdown occurred, an over-worked maintenance type would be summoned into the Comm Center to get the station working again – or replaced - ASAP. I don't recall ever seeing a happy technician during the month or so I worked there. I got the distinct impression that the technician hated me silently and collectively: the F-ing NEW GUY.

The Specialist 5th Class who oversaw my initial Comm Center floor orientation had a hawkish nose, a pencil-thin moustache, and a no-nonsense manner about him. I strived to play the game his way, but it didn't take long for my creative mind to get me into trouble. It all started when one of our distant links "dropped out" in the midst of a message I was sending them.

This was a common phenomenon in electronic communication, especially if the sun was acting up. Solar flares raised holy havoc with all-things-radio. During periods of solar instability, we were challenged to stay linked with our various islands of humanity. If any part of a message was skipped for even a second, our nervous flow of data ceased, and an extroverted stream of unreadable garbage ensued.

Immediate steps had to be taken to reestablish the link, and I was right on it. First I sent them a test strip. This was always the same, and it played in a loop. *Now is the time for every good man to come to the aid of their country* (or) *The quick brown fox jumped over the lazy dog's back.* Being made of paper, the test strips wore out over time. It was up to the 72B20s to stay ahead of the problem and keep a fresh test strip handy; if he was doing nothing else. It had been slow, in fact, so I undertook the job of poking up a new test strip moments before. However, I was bored by the same ol' same ol', so as I started poking that old tired expression onto the new strip, I decided to spice it up a little: *The quick brown fox jumped over the lazy dog's back. Go fox go!* Much better, I thought. Something original for a change.

Hardly two minutes elapsed and the Shift Supervisor was in my face but good. The distant link's shift supervisor happened to be on the other end of my creative test strip, and neither he nor my boss was happy about it. *Who are you to change the way things are done? Tear that %$#@ strip to bits and do as you are told*, he shouted. Sheesh. No sense of humor, I sulked. And so it went.

The next day off I happened upon a nicely typed notice tacked high on the bulletin board just inside the door of our unit's Enlisted Men's Club: "Wanted – Asst. Mgr. Experience desired. Part-time pay - $1.00/hour. See SGT Morris." Needing the extra income, I applied. Describing my (Neff's Drive In) night-manager experience, I signed my name and left my room number.

The EM Club rocked around the clock. With the Unit's work shifts rotating every eight hours, that meant there were always plenty of soldiers off duty. Our Commanding Officer wanted the Club open for them. Else they were likely to head for the bars downtown!

Card tables, pinball machines, a Ping Pong table, mixed drinks, cold beer, a loud, rocking Juke Box and three coin-operated slot machines kept two or three Thai bartenders busy serving drinks, selling coins, keeping things tidy. Drinks were cheap and live entertainment was free.

There was always a Master-at-Arms on duty to keep rowdies under control and to verify any jackpots the slots paid out. There were about a dozen card tables scattered throughout the club that were usually occupied for hours with friendly card games or very serious chess matches. There was even a small stage set up with brightly colored lights for the occasional live band.

I was a chess player in those days, or so I thought. There were a few guys in the unit – I think they were linguists - who studied the chess masters and would usually waste no time trouncing an amateur - unless they felt like delaying the inevitable bloodbath until the Mess Hall doors opened. [Black Queen to White King's P2: **CHECK** and **MATE**. Let's go eat!]

Meanwhile, my work shift went from *swings* to *mids*; we headed to work before midnight and flopped back in the sack well after sunup. Sleep during the day was nearly impossible; the heat in Bangkok was oppressive, unless the monsoons were in effect, or one had a fan in the room. No money for a fan on a PFC's pay of $96.00 a month. Unless you hit a jackpot in the EM Club, of course. Fat chance of that happening.

A new Comm Center guy normally earns his Specialist 4th Class patch [Pay Grade E4] by the time he's been overseas a couple of months. I sewed my SP4 patches on sooner, having garnered an E2 rating in Basic Training. Recognition for leadership, and a few more bucks.

o   o   o   o   o

So here I am back on the Comm Center floor and the brand-new, never ironed SP4 patches on my olive drab sleeves were the topic of conversation. Tradition required your buddies to hammer them onto your arms - *so they'll stick*. Any excuse to **pop** someone. Some guys went overboard, of course. Working a shift with bruised and battered arms didn't help much.

Naturally, when the Army pays a man to be a *Specialist*, he has to perform. The onus is on him to buckle up and handle the floor unassisted on his first solo shift. "Don't screw up. Keep up with the flow. Handle a crisis or two and keep your head on your shoulders."

At the time of his choosing, the Shift Supervisor signaled the other Comm Center guys to clear the Floor. I was actually on my own for a few minutes before I realized everyone was gone. I knew that the Supervisor sometimes monitored the floor from an adjacent wing of the building. If the poo-poo ever hit the spinning blades, the SP5s would come running and restore order.

My test of manhood couldn't have come at a worse time. Mosquitos had been chewing on my hide for days prior, so I hadn't been getting much sleep. I had also devoted a lot of energy at the EM Club, making deposits from the slots and partying with SGT Morris in his private office.

It has been a long time since all this happened, but as I recall, I was less than three minutes into my first solo Floor exercise when one of our machines began spewing garbage profusely. The noise level went up twenty percent. I stopped what I was working on and initiated contact in the clear.

I must be evasive about what happened next so I don't spend the rest of my life in an uncomfortable cell in Leavenworth. I put a test strip into the machine, and as *the quick brown fox* went clicking merrily along, I waited for the party at the other end to give me a green light.

No sooner had I turned around, another island in our link began spewing garbage way off to the left. The noise level went up another twenty percent. Dashing over yonder, I did my thing. In a minute, I restored open commo with them then and crossed back over to the encrypting side of the room to make the necessary adjustments.

It was during this adjustment phase that my normally dependable right hand grabbed ahold of something I shouldn't have touched. With a snap of the wrist, I knocked out commo to another island that had been flowing along at max speed, no thanks to me.

No sooner had I done that, the corresponding island's machine in the center of the room began spewing paper, absolutely covered with gibberish. Now it was noisier than hell! In five minutes, I had managed to lose three islands in the military stream. I was like some man-caused solar flare, knocking myself out! Now things were f-ed up but good. But did I care? Not all that much. From where I laid kicking and screaming on the cold linoleum floor, that Comm Center job was **way** too much for me.

The frigid floor was a hard, slick surface; the suitable platform for yours truly to make like a *Pendejo*. I had myself a well-deserved nervous breakdown. With plenty of energetic tantrum-style leg-kicking and copious cursing of my military job and whomever on Earth could hear me.

Pulling hard at the fresh stitches on my SP4 patch, I almost ripped off my left sleeve when the frowning Shift Supervisor's face came into view overhead. He was glaring at me as though I was a 150-lb. pubic hair, besmirching his precious *Floor*. Man, did I ever hate that job.

Every now and then in this journey called life, Captain Methane collapses into a morass of manure, only to come rising right back up through the fertilizer, covered in rose petals. I am able to say this because – as if by some miracle and practically overnight - SGT Morris got sacked by the Colonel [for having too much fun] and since yours truly was the only other military man who knew the combination to the safe and was versed in *alcohol inventory*, I got the Club Manager's job! No more Comm Center for me. SGT Morris was back on the Floor!

Along with my new *civilian status* came a promotion to Acting SGT E5. The impact of this bit of luck was: a new air conditioned apartment just down the street where all the E5s and above were housed; fewer in-rank inspections; dining with the Officers and NCOs; and a much shorter line at pay call. Perhaps the best part of the job was "Janet," the Club's bilingual Thai employee who worked as our accountant. She balanced our financial records and prepared all our official documents, which I signed. I really didn't have much to do but listen to Chopin, Paganini, and the Beatles on the phonograph and enjoy the delicious Thai fruit Janet purchased from the street vendors.

True to his word, my Army recruiter couldn't have steered me any straighter. I lucked out and turned an unpleasant assignment into a great nine-to-five job and went on to flight school a year later. Near the end of training, my color vision *narrowly* passed the Army Flight Physical Exam's minimum, the *Farnsworth Lantern!*

KUNG FU SKIP

Alcohol and Sauerkraut on the Fly

Camp Enari, on the outskirts of Pleiku in the Central Highlands of Vietnam's II Corps area, is where I performed my duties, in 1969, for the US Army's Fourth Infantry Division. As a Huey pilot, I was honored to be flying at one time or another for either "A" Company's *Blackjacks* or "B" Company's *Gambler Guns*. Most of us young Warrant Officers were housed down the hillside, in what was referred to as "The Ghetto."

Camp Enari had once been an Army of the Republic of Vietnam [ARVN] military compound, and had long rows of barracks lined up four-abreast to house all the pilots. Over time - by scrounging wooden packing crates from thousands of 2.75-inch rocket boxes - resourceful helicopter jockeys fabricated themselves some custom-made hooches. Nothing fancy, but we were far better off than many others In Country who slept in foxholes, or eight to a tent.

There was no such thing as a flush toilet on Post that I recall, unless General Pepke had one. Every other soldier relied on the standard primitive facilities, which were a little further down the hill from the Ghetto, toward the first row of perimeter barbed wire.

Being an all-male outfit, a concession to practicality was made, in that two each "field-type urinals" were located between each row of hooches. These consisted of perforated 55-gallon metal drums, buried until they were almost flush with the ground. The top of the drum was then capped with screen-door wire, perhaps to keep aviators from falling in. A crude wooden shed was then put up, which gave the loitering pilot a little shade, but only gave a mere suggestion of privacy.

The Ghetto's "hooch maids" - as they were known - were local Vietnamese women, (civilians, we hoped), who arrived every morning Monday through Friday to "washy clothes," make our bunks tidy, and sweep up a little. Off-duty-and-inebriated Warrant Officers were known to ask for *assistance* from passing hooch maids while standing before the mighty screen, downloading.

This "practice" was guaranteed to raise a ruckus every time! More than one Unit actually fashioned special awards out of these well-used screens to decorate designated debauchers, deserving something beyond standard military pomp and circumstance.

Walking up the inclined boardwalk to the east, one would leave The Ghetto and come upon two rows of Commissioned Officers' hooches. Naturally, the "real" officers' quarters were more presentable, carefully laid-out, and quasi-militarily correct - considering this *was* a combat zone.

Being *officers and gentlemen*, a hooch maid was far less likely to see a Real Live Officer (RLO) standing butt-naked before the screen, requesting assistance. RLO is a term Warrant Officers used for commissioned officers.

One of the more celebrated pilots in the Ghetto was a fellow we called "Skip." His real first name was decidedly *German*. His last name was also from a famous German clan, which we shall keep secret; owing to a dastardly deed - yet to be revealed.

Skip and I arrived In Country on virtually the same airplane, so as time passed, it appeared we might just survive to take the *freedom flight* together, back to the World, a term soldiers used to identify the USA.

At around ninety days from DEROS (**D**ate **E**stimated to **R**eturn from **O**ver **S**eas) our next assignment "orders" suddenly appeared. It was a celebrated time to be able to say "**FIGMO**," or, **F**- **I**t, **G**ot **M**y **O**rders, to all the guys still breaking in their boots.

Skip was especially elated to have gotten his assignment-of-choice, an Army Aviation Battalion based in West Germany, near his ancestral homeland. Taking a seat at our table in the Officers Club that evening, he was ecstatic! His German accent resurfaced as he laughed about all the great times ahead, "...far away from all these muddy #@!*% rice paddies and slanty-eyed people," he laughed, "HA HA HAH!" Which made us laugh too, well aware that Skip was rumored to have a secret Vietnamese girlfriend in nearby Pleiku City.

Skip seemed to revel in the fact that most of us would get thirty days "leave," and then go right back to Fort Wolters, Texas, where we would teach rookie candidates how to fly those old piston-powered training helicopters. Try to envision one thousand little bug-smashers, swarming around at the same time!

Practically bent over with joy, Herr Brewmeister stood back up with a fist full of MPC notes, **M**ilitary **P**ayroll **C**urrency, used by our troops in Vietnam, and bought a round of beer. Picking up from where he left off, Skip rubbed in the fact that – after leaving Vietnam - our Huey flying days were probably over. But Skip would be flying armed patrols along the Iron Curtain in the latest version "Mike" model Huey - flying *über Deutschland!* He celebrated his great fortune with many cans of the diminutive Officer's Club's coldest beer, which were usually kind of warm and dented.

As the hour grew late, we slowly wandered outside the O' Club. Skip and several others wobbled around a bit in the dark, adjusting to the darkness, or lighting up cancer sticks and/or heading toward the nearest screen. In this case, it was the RLO's brand-spanking new, freshly buried metal drum.

There it stood - practically unscathed - under a sturdy-looking shed of some kind, designed to hide anyone in the process of downloading. A flawless red metal can half-full of clean sand hung at arm's reach, a neatly stenciled sign on its side said, "Butts."

The lieutenants had worked extra hard to get the spiffy new urinal ready before the evening's gathering. It smelled of fresh paint in the dark and while standing *in position*, one couldn't help but notice the RLOs had come up with some honest, 4-inch-by-4-inch-by-8-foot wood posts, to which were nailed carefully-sawn rocket-box side-partitions.

Whereas, down in The Ghetto, we possessed nothing so *evolved*.

And to one happy-drunk German, the prissy hut was a brazen insult to *him* and *The Ghetto* - and it must **go!** He shouted an oath, advising all us would-be down-loaders to **stand aside!**

Always ready for a good laugh, we standers-by raised very few objections as *Skip-turned-Don-Quixote* challenged the shed with a guttural expletive. He sprang with all the strength his stocky German bod could muster, straight into a near-perfect martial arts flying-side-kick. One had to admire the height and energy a drunken aviator can achieve under these conditions.

Alas, the officers had done a resounding job of packing dirt around the shed's sturdy posts, and the one that Skip's GI boot contacted stood its ground, while the Skipper's beefy leg bones suffered under the physics of a *spiral-compound-fracture*. To soften the blow to Skip's *insult to injury*, we declared him an "Honorable Recipient of the Flying Piss Screen Device," in absentia.

And that's the last we saw of ol' Skip, poor guy! He would spend many painful weeks recovering in a drab, stateside military hospital, so he could return to flight duty. And *gone* was that dream tour in Germany. Someone else would upgrade into that slot. *Kung Fu Skip* would be Texas-based, studying the military Method of Instruction manual and mentally preparing for his first flock of grasshoppers.

DENNY AND THE KEY

Going Green in a Sleek Machine

Denny and yours truly were chopper pilots stationed at a military base in New Mexico. We had recently completed an obligatory twelve-month combat tour of Vietnam. Both of us were slated to be released from the active Army in a few months. You could say we were unwinding from the stress of war, adjusting to life without firearms, without our former love-interests, and living in uniform in a time that gave little credit to The Service.

Dennis, or "Denny" as his friends called him, was freshly separated from his blond Arizona wife – speaking of hippies - and their two young daughters. He put on a carefree face to mask his anguish, but I knew him to be an involuntary divorcee, masquerading as a flamboyant minstrel of a bachelor. His true feelings concerning a dramatic divorce varied from whimsical to mortally crucified, as he lived with traumatic separation from his golden-fleeced females. Apparently, there was a compatibility issue.

I also occupied a shitty little room at the Heartbreak Hotel. This Huey pilot was recovering from a mindblower of a divorce. My pretty former high school sweetheart had - by her silence - created a maddening situation for me while I was overseas in combat mode. The girl I called my wife had abruptly, and completely without explanation, quit writing to me. From one or two letters a day to zero, overnight. Three weeks went by...

To solve this heartbreaking mystery, I returned home on emergency leave two-thirds through my tour, determined to face whatever awaited me. How could a woman abandon her husband while he was away fighting a war? These were impossible thoughts for me to accept.

At long last, came the day of reckoning. Her slick civil attorney pounced on the fact that his client and I had been legally separated the required six months. All that was lacking was my signature on his military waiver.

Hours later, my "dearly beloved" and I sat on adjacent ornate benches in the halls of justice, waiting for our time before the judge. She was defiant yet silent, and wearing no wedding ring. Pulling mine off at the last possible second, I flung it past her in an arc intended to sink it in the nearby brass cuspidor, but I missed. The size-nine gold ring ricocheted off the rim with an awful "crash" and rolled slowly around us in a large, unobserved, wobbling circle, mocking our marriage as it floundered to a stop.

We were standing at last before His Honor, Judge Sanders. His daughter Nell and I used to go roller skating together. My Father and I had refinished several fine pieces of furniture for the Judge in the mid-sixties. Beautiful wood chairs they were, some said to be from the Lincoln Library. His Honor had been pleased with our work, Dad told me.

Judge Sanders frowned as his eyes met mine, recognizing my name. He glanced briefly at the pretty plaintiff and back at me, dressed in Army uniform. Making no comment, Judge Sanders took up his black pen and dissolved the paper link that represented our bond. The young woman was now free to change her name back to whatever it was.

The very same thoughtful person called me the next day, leaning on me to pay for the divorce - which occurred on my birthday, as if by design. She hadn't any money, she argued. Her attorney demanded payment, she pressed. "Sure. Just for you." I replied, weary from already losing everything I had. Then it was back into the long, crowded airliner and off to Vietnam with Mr. Wingo.

So it might come as no surprise - after all the levity Denny and I had experienced - the two of us were looking for a remedy to our after-hour negative mood swings. We didn't cater much to booze, you see. An official function at the "O" Club, sure. A toast to welcome the new guy, "adios" to the old guy; one must mingle, after all. A cold beer or two to wash the dust down, perhaps. But after bingeing on Jack Daniels & Coke so many times in Vietnam, we were mutually persuaded of the axiom, "With booze, you lose."

Denny and I had our ears to the ground for something that would take the edge off of our highly-stimulated-under-financed-testosterone-saturated, temporarily-celibate-but-adventurous pair of chopper pilots. Yet that "something" mustn't leave our quick-thinking, multi-tasking, helicopter-pilot brains with a hangover - so we could shoot straight and fly right the next morning. Ergo the more popular: With dope, there is hope.

We could have launched a day earlier, had we known the good news. Our reliable connection called Saturday afternoon from El Paso with remedy in hand: "Come and get it," she giggled, coughing hoarsely as she delivered the long-awaited line.

By the time I cleaned up and marched down the concrete steps in front of the Holloman Air Force Base BOQ, the sun had sunk. That was fine with me - I loved to drive my new machine at night. "She" was a sleek, dark blue, 1970 Corvette Stingray Sport Coupe, with 350 horses under the hood. She was well equipped - including a luxurious, padded black leather and mesh cockpit to slide into. My ride was financed, to help me get over her.

Donning a pair of kid-leather driving gloves, I snapped the seat belt into its receiver. Easing the clutch pedal to the floor, I cranked the key forward. An abrupt, throaty chorus erupted under the hood and the cockpit rumbled merrily along. Alas, she had an automatic choke; ergo my Stingray was a cold-hearted bitch, warming up.

Pulling the headlight switch out two clicks, the instrument panel lit up. I heard the vacuum assisted headlights unstow, confirming low beams parked in cruise position.

I eased the syncro into first gear while holding her horses at bay. Rumbling out of the BOQ parking lot, I headed eastward along one of Holloman's residential thoroughfares.

A few F-4 Phantom jocks were still out having their evening run, lit up by my headlights. Amber running lamps aglow, there was nary a speck of dust on my gleaming road machine. Day or night, the Stingray was a head-turner. She loved the attention, too.

Warmed up at last, I tapped the gas pedal, observing her antsy RPM needle as it dropped back to something reasonable. Once toasty, her problematic choke quit interfering with throttle input. I kept her under 25 all the way out the gate, where a white-helmeted Airman MP saluted the diminutive blue sticker on the Corvette's gorgeous wrap-around chrome bumper. I toed the high beams into service and sped off into the night.

Shifting through the Hurst four-speed was a G-loaded joy, as I finally left the speed traps of Alamogordo behind, rumbling past Alamo Peak toward High Rolls. Reaching forward with my gloved shifting hand, I flipped the f-ing FM radio off. Every song I ever heard on that damned thing reminded me of someone I badly needed to forget.

Denny was still getting his act together when I pulled in his gravel driveway and up to the old two-room cabin. He had moved here - just off Highway 82 on the long climb to Cloudcroft – soon after Pamela left him. I could hear him placating his two hungry cats as I walked up the dirt path to his door. Cats were all that remained of his family now. Arwen's Brandywine Lady, his energetic purebred Irish Setter pup, had recently run away.

Announcing my arrival, I tossed my overnight bag onto the center of Freeman's king-sized waterbed like a bomb, digging the "splash" it made. Denny ignored my prank, returning my "hello" and noisily finished feeding his famished felines. He gave the cats each a loving rub, saying all the while how he missed his beautiful, red-haired puppy.

When I didn't chime in to his melancholy, he changed the subject by saying "Oh well," and let out a long sigh. Denny was complex. He had wars going on inside his skull that drove him to anxiety and sadness: something that I wanted no part of, on this night of grand adventure. We had been hoping for a brick, and our brick awaited, two hours away.

Used to hurried turn-arounds, Freeman had at least managed to perform "the four S's[2]" in short order. He was soon wistfully counting out his half of the $150.00 investment in tonight's illegal marijuana run. With my matching funds, we aimed to score a kilo in old El Paso from a reliable source, before the night was over. This was a first for either of us.

Cruising south down Highway 54 to El Paso in the dark of night, billions of stars twinkled overhead in the moonless New Mexico sky. Freeman was off on some cosmic tangent, entertaining me with periodic masterful storytelling. I could hardly keep my eyes on the road; it was so inspirational to see the Milky Way in such clarity. Spirits were high, yet this was the low-risk half of the trip. Bringing the key "home" would be much riskier.

---

[5] The US Army taught us in basic training to "**S**have **S**hit **S**hower and **S**hine!"

The two-lane blacktop to El Paso was mostly straight, but there were sometimes large terrapins wandering across; at least two sudden decelerations for cattle guards and/or sharp turns, and a constant risk of coyotes and castrated cattle complicated our cruise.

We had come this way before in the Vette, to attend a Three Dog Night concert in El Paso, my first-ever live rock concert experience. The Armory was packed. We sat way in the back, dressed like hippies, pretending to be "free" that night.

But it was easy to spot a couple of military guys with our short haircuts and trimmed facial hair. Lots of stares from casual pot smokers, thinking we might be narcs? The music was great, though, and the talented band played every famous tune with amazing fidelity.

At the end of our two-hour drive, we pulled into Joy's narrow driveway. One of her two cats glared at our brightly lit, rumbling intrusion and disappeared into the hedgerow. Killing the Stingray's engine, I swung the sports car's door open wide, as did Freeman. We rose slowly and began stretching our cramped legs, our talking creating puffs of fog. Feeling the cold El Paso night air, we were reminded to grab our jackets from the small "luggage area" behind the seats.

Walking straight over to Joy's kitchen door, we stopped briefly to admire a stunted-looking two-foot cannabis[6] plant growing right outside her kitchen window. "Pretty casual," we chuckled, considering Texas' harsh marijuana laws in 1970[7], but that was the avant-garde Ms. Fox for you.

Joy dabbled in professional drafting in those days, a crafty woman four years my senior. She was merrily draping a few of her latest tie-dye t-shirts on the chair backs when we waltzed in.

She sported one of her own creations, and with no bra underneath, she had Freeman's rapt attention. He was hardly able to take his eyes off of her colorful, shocking, concentric designs - until she suddenly produced the brick, that is. "Tried a pinch already," she giggled, giving us the ol' thumbs up. "It's **FAR OUT**, man!"

Ms. Fox had recently made pals with a certain someone with diplomatic immunity, who regularly crossed the US - Mexico border. That made for

---

[6] The 2.2 pounds of *cannabis sativa*, soaked in Coca-Cola and pressed into a lunch-pail sized block of leaves, buds, seeds, and stems – allowed to dry, and tightly wrapped in newspaper for retail. Also a *brick*, or *a key*.

[7] Penalty for simple possession could result in sentences of twenty years or more.

party favors in the trunk, or whatever. The kilo of grass had come from the Interior, that was all she knew. I didn't ask her if she was making any money on the deal and didn't really want to know. I handed Sis the cash and gave her a big hug for helping her brother and a friend out.

Denny got busy rolling one for the road while I negotiated with Joy for two of her "most bizarre" t-shirts - ten bucks a pop. Freeman, fresh out of cash for some reason, would reimburse me later for his. After a stimulating round of hot Ginseng tea and a few more laughs, we bid adieu to friendly Fox and moved our act back outside.

Between our bulky jackets, the brick and the shirts, the Corvette's luggage space was fairly maxed out. We cloaked the critical package with our jackets, but immediately noticed its pungent aroma when we closed the Stingray's doors. No hiding that smell!

Joy's cats scattered like frightened quail when the bitch fired back up, her engine warm still from the drive over, her Lake pipes sounding like she could rumble sweet music forever. We blew Joy one last kiss, backed out to the street, and headed for New Mexico.

Freeman waited until we reached the long straight stretch out past Fort Bliss to light up his joint. Cracking the Corvette's window just so, we let the smoke slip out venturi fashion while engaging in commentary worthy of a Cheech and Chong essay. We did not get pulled over or anal-probed, and by the time we arrived back at Denny's cabin, we were feeling no pain. No bitches were mentioned and the world was sane for a moment.

We were both amazed at the amount of work it took to break the kilo down into halves. It had formed a hard green chunk for the most part, and that took lots of hands-on kneading to break the stems and seeds loose from the good stuff. Once we got ourselves a good-sized bag of pure green flowers, we stashed the rest in Quaker oatmeal boxes.

All told we had about ¾ pound apiece once we were done. It was seedy stuff, but that helps establish that the product was mature at harvest time, and there was never any complaint as to its potency. The best part of the deal was, we were able to whip up a large batch of chocolate-walnut tokeless brownies. Didn't actually measure the active ingredient – we had so much at the time; it didn't seem excessive when we dumped it in the mixer. We baked and froze over four-dozen of them. Our hope was that one brownie would produce the desired effect.

NOT! Way too much cannabis! A single brownie produced psychedelic experiences lasting an hour or longer; followed by the munchies, then blissful slumber. The key was to eat only one-fourth. We discovered that like guinea pigs do: experiment, experiment!

PLAN "B" FROM DEEPER ARIZONA

Liberated Lumber from Under the Lama

Carefully closing the thin aluminum door to my ancient Airstream, I wanted my pregnant mate to continue slumbering while I took off for work. The trailer's creaky fold-a-step groaned and squawked under one size-ten while my other boot sank into the gooey North Rim Arizona mud, a lasting reminder to round up something for a porch.

We had just arrived the day before at this chopper pilot's job-of-a-lifetime, a July-to-December project working in and around the Grand Canyon National Monument. I brought my young Mexican bride and a motorcycle along for the fun. Pushing the Yamaha away from the campground, I flipped the key, clicked 'er into second gear and bump-started it for the short but exhilarating ride to the helicopter's LZ.

Today, the customer's head honcho was meeting us with a truckload of lumber. "Honcho Harry" was ten miles away – across the Heart of the Canyon on the South Rim – as the crow flies. Harry had purchased the lumber at a mill in neighboring Flagstaff. Joining me for the flight across the Canyon was "Wally," our construction foreman.

We had permission from the NPS to stage a lift operation, using their South Rim maintenance yard. We brought along two nylon choker-straps, a remote hook, and a one-hundred-twenty-five-foot long-line to rig the 1200-lb. load.

"Plan A" was to fly the lumber back across the canyon, where carpenters would build a replacement helipad on an incline near the North Rim's Bright Angel Falls. The ancient helipad currently in use was literally falling apart.

Flying a turbine-powered helicopter straight across the most incredible landscape on planet Earth for the first time should be experienced in the

SA-315B Lama, whose simplistic glass canopy lets it happen. At 8,500 feet, the world is indeed your oyster.

My wife, on the other hand, wouldn't fly across the Grand Canyon with me for all the Pesos in Puerto Rico.

The NPS maintenance yard was rectangular in shape and had a windsock. We landed without incident. There was adequate room for the sling operation, and then some. The lot was paved, which reduced the dust factor considerably. Assisting in rigging the load, Harry and Wally correctly applied the choker belts around the 20-foot long bundle and inserted the choker-belt-ends into the jaw of our fresh-out-of-the-box remote hook.

I safety-wired the steel clevises and checked both hooks' dual-releases. The "remote hook" was an older-version cargo hook, shipped to us by our friendly maintenance department. It looked kind of old, but showed little mechanical wear – other than an opaque inspection window near the knurled knob. One couldn't begin to see through it.

Power lines punctuated the yard's west-end departure. Lacking sufficient "runway" from the west end, I made like an 800 horsepower hummingbird over the load, taking all the slack out of the line and belts; reefing the lumber slowly into the air. I hovered carefully eastbound until the load settled due to the tailwind factor. Twice more I picked the load up and hovered downwind until I could go no further east.

Turning her nose west, I dialed in max allowable pitch and immediately enjoyed improved lift performance, heading into a gentle breeze. Helicopter and heavy load started up slowly, climbing toward the power lines.

My French flying machine performed flawlessly as the cellulose sailed past my nervous customers, up and over the power lines with room to spare. I radioed my departure-with-sling-load over Unicom, announcing my right climbing turnout over the South Rim's awesome Abyss. What a view!

Flittering along a mile above the mighty Colorado River, I checked the load, and then scanned for traffic as I turned slowly upstream toward Phantom Ranch and the confluence of Bright Angel Creek.

It was along this incredible vista that my remote hook decided it wasn't locked shut.

I felt an abrupt lurch upward, my three-bladed aerial crane's reaction to losing the heavy cargo.

Banking right for an eyeful, air rushed through the open cockpit as I observed the load fall away in slow motion. The bundle did a slow roll, the belts began loosening. Their girth expanded as the beams and boards began fluttering in the accelerating gale. The frenzied load suddenly exploded into scores of tumbling wooden bombs, heading in all directions while rotating horizontally. Out-of-control combines, spinning their way down into hell. [Are those tiny dots in the river, rafters?]

Immediately upstream from where the load exploded, I spot a sightseeing helicopter, a little ahead of me but half-a-mile lower. Fortunately, the Jet Ranger is headed away from all of this – but who might be trailing him? I shuddered to think.

"Mayday Mayday Mayday!" I radioed. *"A load of lumber is falling into the Grand Canyon, one-half-mile upstream from the Abyss! Heads up!"* My long-line trailing me, I made a wide 360-degree turn in an attempt to track the debris and yellow choker belts as jetsam floated, flittered and spun. Some crashed dramatically into the roiling red Colorado River's treacherous Lava Falls!

Climbing dejectedly back toward my starting point, I had a good idea where most of the scattered lumber might be found, and I knew darned well the NPS would see to it that we picked up every little piece. This became "Plan B."

Following my shut-down at the maintenance yard, Harry, Wally, and the local NPS pilot listened intently as I reported the incident, emphasizing that the remote hook had been under a 1200 lb. strain three separate times before taking the load aloft. It had opened of its own accord, and as far as I was concerned, it was going back into the box, right back where it came from. We'd never be able to trust it again. (They readily agreed!)

The next morning we were in the air by 07:00 in order to fly six men and some cargo nets to the sultry bottom of the Canyon. An NPS engineer came with us to witness the cleanup. In mid-July, it was a hot, sweaty, team effort to locate all the boards and splinters and pitch them into designated piles. I then flew around with long-line and swivel hook, picking up the far-away net-loads and consolidating those into one large pile for the final load. Destination: the North Rim's scrap-yard.

The eight-inch-by-eight-inch-by-sixteen-foot posts fell like bombs and had fared the worst, but the four-inch-by-twelve-inch lumber "auto rotated" into the 500 million year-old Navajo limestone, surviving with minimal damage. Plan B was a "wrap" by 09:00, but not before reaching 34 degrees Celsius. We climbed for the North Rim, just in time for breakfast.

Lourdes was awake and glad to see us back at the Airstream. She noted Wally helping me offload large pieces of battered wood from his truck, remnants that I planned to saw up into a new porch.

"*Is that for our porch-ito?*" she inquired in English. Drawing me aside, she asked in Spanish, "*Where did you get this ugly, old stuff?*"

Thankfully, Wally had a sense of humor and chuckled as I answered, "That's a long story, Lulú. We can tell you all about it over some coffee!"

THE CAPTAIN IN GRASS PANTS

Shopping with Nancy, a Melodrama.

It doesn't really matter when this happened, because a guy like me could probably do what I am about to demonstrate at any appliance store in America today. Well, not the one in Grants Pass, Oregon. They learned about helicopter pilots thirty years ago.

Three decades ago and forty miles from the appliance store, I was working near my rustic "A" frame cabin along the West Fork of the Illinois River. It was raining as usual, a chilly November afternoon in your average helicopter firefighter's "off season." My work on the savage brush pile was done. I slogged back toward the cabin and the addictive warmth of the old wood stove.

The relentless rain had begun to wear down my rusty New Mexican optimism for the sun's belated return to Illinois Valley. Strolling into my humble ten by twelve-foot cabin, hunger struck as I peeled off my stiff rain gear and stomped some of the mud off of my Herman's Survivors on the gorilla-proof floor mat. I methodically tossed a smooth red log into "Tin Man," my tall, brick-lined wood stove.

The yawning cylindrical top-loading stove swallowed the heavy Madrone log and showered me with hot sparks in return. Putting out a stubborn shirt-sleeve fire, I pressed the tape player's "on" button, remembering too late that the cabin's batteries were dead because I hadn't run the generator. Now I couldn't run the generator; I used the last of the gasoline on the brush pile. Sheesh!

Peeking into the ice chest, I examined my prospects for dinner. One bruised apple, two slices of bacon and one Henry's, all floating around in what used to be a big block of ice.

Another check of the cupboard to confirm the old can of Spam sat undisturbed. No way.

Heading down the winding path to where the Power Wagon snoozed, I found myself weakening to the call of the city, where laundry and pizzas shouted for my quarters and greenbacks. Warming up the cold-blooded Dodge, I loaded the dirty laundry and empty gas jugs for a ten-minute drive to town.

An hour or so later, while the dry-cycle was doing its thing, I trashed the empty pizza box and hopped over to the hardware store with a short list of stuff I needed for a Hobbit-sized cabinet project. And what do you know, I ran into Nancy Brown.

Nancy is a lively local elementary school teacher, the wife of Cave Junction's very own high school wrestling coach – and my smokejumper pal – Wes Brown. Nancy let it be known that she was on her way to "Grass Pants," as we called Grants Pass, the nearest "big town[8]," a half-hour's drive north of Cave Junction.

It was customary among our fire-fighting friends to offer rides to Grass Pants, gas prices being what they were, and most of us small-towners were always looking for better deals in the big city. Nancy was all excited, saying that she was going shopping for a new refrigerator for the rambling log house she and her hubby built near the smoke jumper base. She was going alone, while Wes caught up on firewood for their epic fireplace.

Realizing I had nothing better to do, I found myself swept up by her enthusiasm. She might need a hand loading it up, anyhow, so I agreed to go along for the ride. Within minutes, I was able to wrap up my shopping and load the Dodge with clean, hot, dry laundry. The stinky gas jugs would have to wait.

Right on time, Mrs. Brown swung her four-wheel drive pickup into the muddy lot as I locked up the Power Wagon and climbed in her rig for the afternoon drive to Grass Pants.

I was soon swapping cabin-construction stories with Nancy while she navigated the rain-slick meandering highway. Before I knew it, we were walking through the well-illuminated glass entrance to "Appliance City[9]," a fairly large venue known to shave prices; like today's **Big Winter Sale**," for instance.

---

8 National Park Service
9 Not the real name of the store.

Salesmen just love to see smiling people walk through the door, so they naturally latched on to Nancy before we got three steps toward the merchandise. Standing there in my helicopter ball cap, I was decidedly less interested; it was Nancy's money that was on the line, not mine. I was just there to help. "Just shopping," she said, and brushed by them.

As the greedy sales types backed off and waited for the right moment, Nancy soon narrowed her search down to one of the more expensive models in the back of the store. Her body English apparently gave her selection away, because a white-shirted salesman suddenly appeared beside the chosen metal monolith. Leaning up against it like Fred Astaire, he purred, "Nice choice, Ma'am." He centered his narrow necktie while quoting the make and model, capacity, and guarantee. Praising the unit's unique features, he suggested that Mrs. Brown was about to take possession of the last such article in Siskiyou County.

"Take for example, the new **miracle plastic** used in the construction of this spacious vegetable bin," he needlessly explained, for I felt Nancy had already decided to buy the beauty. The salesman sat the empty vegetable bin down on the white tiled showroom floor with its flat, clear plastic lid locked in place. "It is so strong, you can jump up and down on it," he said quite matter-of-factly.

Invitations such as these come along so rarely in life; a man has a better chance of being struck by lightning. You might understand then, why this alert chopper pilot took the salesman's statement as a challenge, not just an idle sales-pitch. Up I sprang to a three-foot hover, coming down hard with my mud-encrusted, Vibram-soled Hermans like a diesel-powered pile driver.

The noise created by the exploding vegetable bin inside the large appliance store has been stored inside my audio-memory banks all these years, lying in wait for such times as when I am most susceptible, like between the last few pages of a good mystery novel.

As Nancy and the now speechless salesman stood looking at the shattered debris afoot, I scanned to my right, tracing a belated clattering sound. Another wide-eyed sales-guy stooped to pick up a fist-sized busted plastic shard that made it all the way across the store.

"In all my years of selling refrigerators…" our salesman began mumbling, as Nancy Brown and I stepped slowly away from the miracle plastic vegetable bin, giving the traumatized sales clerk an opportunity for some closure.

With eyes red from laughing all the way home, Nancy finally dropped me off at the laundromat, where she waved a cheery goodbye. She would look elsewhere for her reefer, and she never asked me to go appliance shopping with her again!

THE DEMO FLIGHT

"Punch it," says he!

When I returned from six months of helicoptering in the Peruvian jungle, several tiny subdural creatures were still chewing their way into my thick Okie hide. And there was this incredible *mold thingie* growing on my right foot that threatened to take over my loafer – and McMinnville, too – if I didn't find a cure.

To lift my spirits and distract me while I healed up, the BCO (Big Cheese in Operations) sent me to that wonderful helicopter school over in Texas. You know the one, where Bell Helicopter teaches you all the systems, checks you out on the controls, and sends you off in your brand new twin-engine Bell 212. Sweet!

It was my pleasure to fly our new machine cross-country to southwestern Oregon, just in time to start a new five-month US Forest Service Region VI Rappel Crew fire contract near Cave Junction. My new base of operations was none other than the Illinois Valley Airport, historically the home of the fabled Siskiyou Smoke Jumpers.

Having honed my external load skills on the preceding jungle job, my confidence was high in returning to fire duty at the controls of the new Bell. To satisfy the terms of the contract, though, my relief pilot and I had to demonstrate to the Forest Service that we could hover 250 feet over a designated point – with precision – while three pairs of rookie rappellers dropped quickly down twin beefy nylon ropes via *Sky Genie* descent control devices.

The precision part of the flying was no big deal, really, once you learned to lock in a 45 degree angle off the helicopter's nose and transpose that 45 degrees downward to the *focal point*. I found that pine cones, tree tops, large branches and the like worked best for overlapping focal points.

So oriented, the 212 is visually locked into position as the "Rope Sliders" hook up their harnesses to the ropes. Making their way off the cargo deck, they maneuver down the slick, folding-aluminum "beaver" slides, past the helicopter's skids and down they go, 200 feet – landing gently within a ten-foot diameter clearing on the ground.

Ahh, this is great, I'm thinkin'! My shiny new Bell performs as advertised, making oodles of power and hovering happily, whether heavily loaded with rappellers or not.

We deftly insert a six man rappel team into the designated cathedral of trees, lower their saws and other gear to the ground, drop the dangling nylon lines and take off – making it look like we'd been practicing for days.

As the sun sank toward the treetops, our festive crew slapped each other on the back and gathered their gear. We were about to call it a day when one of the *Feds* running the show asked our Helitack Manager for "a *demo* of the helicopter's water bucket."

You know, a *demonstration*. Just to verify that the water bucket works? Not that the pilot would have any difficulty demonstrating its use – after putting on such an impressive rappeller insertion just moments ago. Just a formality, but one that needs to be checked off the ol' clipboard.

*Ahh, this is even **better***, I thought. More external load work! Nobody onboard the helicopter to annoy the pilot; just the Captain, breathing in the intoxicating smell of brand new radios, fresh paint and upholstery, enjoying the view through unblemished clear plastic in each and every window. *This isn't work, this is fun!*

Strapped once again into the right seat, I note the Helitack Manager out front, signaling that the 300-gallon "Griffith" water bucket has been hooked up electrically and mechanically. He gives me the "open" and "shut" signs. [Note: This was in the days before water-bucket gate-switches were moved to the collective pitch control.] In response, I tilt the *China hat* atop the cyclic stick aft for "open," and the other way for "close." The Manager verifies the gate is operational.

Now for the water bucket demo! It has been over a year since my last bucket work, but it all comes rushing back to me as I hover smartly over to the Smoke Jumper's favorite practice pond. Thumbing the China hat, I remember to reopen the bucket's gate. Observing the action below via a large convex cargo mirror, the ship descends vertically near the shoreline, where the Griffith bucket plops, then sinks sluggishly into the dark green water.

Hovering directly over the sunken vessel, I trigger the gate shut. Scanning between the mirror and all the gauges, I centered the ship over the load and summoned the horses, adding left pedal to keep the nose into the wind – what little wind there was. I wondered if all the hole-plugs were installed in the bucket. We don't want it too heavy, after all; this is just a demo flight.

Torqued out. In the yellow, temp-wise, producing whitecaps, a gale and lots of noise. Slowly the bucket emerges from the deep. Yes, she is full to the top! I hold red line torque, ease in forward cyclic as the twin *N1* gas producer needles nervously hunt and check one another within their narrow green arcs. RPM dual-tach is in the green! The bloated barrel plows through the pond as we gain speed and inch upward. My right hand's third finger rests against the cargo-hook release button, in case we lose power.

We only had a few minutes left per Forest Service daylight rules, so the man in forest green attire emphasized this would be a *"short"* demonstration. As I gained altitude, he called me over the FM ground frequency to *make a short pattern* and return to drop water on the designated tree, center stage and about one hundred feet from where all the Smoke Jumpers and the Rappel Crew were standing.

The subject pine tree waits patiently for me as I turn left and line up for a slow moving but precise salvo of water, the release of which will be ordered by the Fed with the radio. There's little or no wind again, so the rotors and I have to work harder to sustain the heavy bucket just beyond the pine tree's uppermost needles.

Ahhh, nuts, the blinding sun is right square in my eyes as I blink and try to stay over the spot, waiting for the command.

"Punch it!" he yells, and I did.

But instead of having my *skilled* right thumb on the *China hat*, my *stupid* third finger was still on the cyclic's *cargo-hook release-button*. The ship instantly lurched upward and the bucket streaked downward, shearing off tree limbs as it fell.

Ahhhh crap!! I thought, and then: *will it survive the fall??*

As my eyeballs grew larger, the expensive, circular Griffith bucket grew quickly smaller in the mirror until it abruptly hit the ground – level – at the base of the big pine. It was spontaneously reduced to a humongous, two-dimensional, four-pedaled, orange rubber daffodil, with wire cables in disarray, tree limbs and pond water flowing everywhere.

Yours truly forgot all about the sun in his eyes, his itchy jungle rot, and all his other problems about then. He did his best to remember how to fly a helicopter as he maneuvered awkwardly toward the pond, to the designed Landing Zone – where he bounced and cursed and bounced like a wounded duck, trying to land while reprimanding himself loudly, off mike.

After my short confession that I had simply pushed the wrong button, the Fed put away his clipboard and the Crew helped put the big bird to bed while their pilot made for the telephone. It would be an overnighter to McMinnville for him, to trade his busted bucket in for a new one.

And to write on the chief pilot's blackboard a hundred times, *"I will never, ever…"*

182 TO RED BLUFF

And Secret Weapon Number Two

When the boss discovered I was planning a getaway to Oregon with my family of three, he reminded me that there was a potentially big helicopter parts customer doing business a couple of hours' drive from my destination. Being the clever man he is, Clair Merryweather [aka "Stormy"] suggested I put his 1958 Cessna 182A to use and kill two birds with one stone.

It was a great idea, because I already flew "the company plane," mainly as transportation to some of Western Helicopter's remote contracts. My pretty Mexican wife, Lourdes, and I had contemplated driving to Oregon, but the Cessna would save us at least three days of road time. We could always borrow some wheels once we got to Cave Junction, our destination. It was a no-brainer!

Loading up the Cessna at Rialto Airport [L67] included a box of diapers for our two-year-old son, Robert, who was about to take his first cross-country airplane ride. My wife seemed to be onboard for this flight, although she had been a reluctant passenger on more than one of the helicopter rides I had shared with her during three years of wedded bliss. She put on her most courageous face and settled into the right front seat with Robert in her lap, as I pulled the wheel chocks and climbed in.

The Cessna was gassed to the max and loaded with all our gear, though it was not quite grossed out. Impressing Lourdes with my familiarity of fixed-wing aircraft – as well as being an experienced commercial chopper pilot – I breezed through the start-up procedure without the aid of my checklist, saving precious seconds; making her feel more comfortable?

Mashing the start button, the reliable six-banger Continental fired right up, as our chief pilot, Pete Gillies marched past our left wing tip. At which point, the engine's short fuel line ran dry, and the engine chugged to a halt. Pete let out a cowboy's **yee-haww** at the sudden silence, reminding a certain big-shot helicopter pilot that he had failed to point his fuel selector ***arrow*** – located on the floor between the front seats – to the ***on*** position.

Brilliant! Lovely Lourdes looked me over and closely followed my right hand as I corrected my omission, taking the error in stride while she placated our antsy son in her arms. With the engine restarted, I waved *"Thank you, buddy"* to my instructor and taxied out to the active for take-off. It was a warm morning but a routine rollout to take-off, and off we went, into the blue.

It is here that I pause to assure my readers the whole trip from this point on went quite well, thank you. We landed and refueled in Red Bluff, making our final destination in Oregon on time. The Siskiyou County Airport [SIY] had a secure tie-down for the Cessna, and with many good friends around, we had wheels whenever we needed them.

We attended a BIG "toga party" on the southern slopes of Lone Mountain, complete with scores of firefighter friends; a rock band; a neighborly hot tub; a stuffed yearling pig, roasted in a pit; and a big king salmon, also roasted in the ground. Beer and wine flowed freely, children sang and played, and little Robert ran up and down the hill in his little white toga outfit, having a blast.

Oh, and that sales call *Stormy* wanted me to make? Yours truly drove to Cottage Grove and within a few minutes got a handshake deal – on the spot – from our new parts customer, which pleased the boss to be sure. Things couldn't really have gone better on our little voyage, with one exception. That first fuel stop we made, in Red Bluff?

There ***was*** a teeny problem there.

Red Bluff [RBL] was around 500 air miles, or about as far as I dared fly, considering my inexperienced passengers. Chopper pilots are used to stretching our legs on a regular basis, too. I was somewhat familiar with their 5700 foot airstrip, as I had landed some civilian Hueys there back in the day we were ferrying frost-protection aircraft for Evergreen Helicopters.

The airfield offered transient tie-down space and a couple of places to buy Av-Gas, back in the summer of 1981. I knew from calling ahead that they had a nice café. After refueling, we could climb out, exercise and enjoy some lunch before the final stretch to Cave Junction.

Selecting FBO's[10] from my Western States Flight Guide, I chose the northern-most operator at the far end of the active, where it would be a snap to land, taxi in and out for fuel, and back to the café.

That was my plan anyway, as I rolled off runway 330, cranked up the manual flaps, popped the side-window open, and taxied to the service ramp – aiming for the Fuel Island. There was a faded Av-Gas sign above the **low lead** hose reel. I tapped the right brake lightly to make a nice easy clockwise turn around the island to point us back the way we came in.

I failed to observe, as I was making the right-hand turn, that one of the FBO's hangar doors was latched open. While the airplane's tail was briefly pointed at the open doorway, the left tire rolled slightly uphill into a shallow drift of sand and our forward momentum stalled.

Meanwhile – in the seat to my right – Lourdes is having issues with baby Robert, whose little ears didn't appreciate our rapid descent from 11,500 feet only moments before. Up there it was cool. Then came that awful ear-popping stuff, all the way down to the sweltering hot airport. He was temporarily inconsolable, perhaps prompting my throttle hand as I revved the engine, gaining enough thrust to ride over the sand with the Cessna's low profile tire.

What I didn't see during throttle-up was the blast of sand and dust which shot underneath the Cessna and straight into the open hangar door. I eased 'er forward a few more feet; locking the brakes; checklist out; everything ***off***.

And there we sat, cooling our jets, when an angry mechanic stomped out of the hangar through the dissipating dust cloud – heading straight in our direction!

By then, Lourdes and I (A) realized our precious son's bowels had moved recently and (B) saw the angry individual coming by the tail in time to grok why he was standing under my left wing, yelling at me about having **an engine on the bench – full of dirt now**, thanks to me.

He looked like he might literally bust a ***gut*** when Lourdes – bless her timing – undid the sticky side-tabs of our wailing baby's dirty diaper and ***voila:*** Robert is doing the **Full Monty**, liberally garnished with what might pass for ***fresh spinach***, from a distance.

---

10   Fixed Base Operators

That did it. The mechanic bolted upright, almost hitting his head on the underside of the wing. Reeling from the vivid imagery and what was wafting freely from the cockpit, he staggered backwards. When I opened my door and stepped out to breathe, he had retreated into the old hangar.

A teenage employee walked out to the pumps a few moments later, a chip off the angry mechanic's old block. He was happy to fill both mains **to the tabs** and take our money. With Robert all cleaned up and hungry, we taxied back to the café for a refreshing lunch. We never heard another syllable from the mechanic.

I've long pondered my fortune at the outcome of this incident, wondering how I got off so easily with the angry mechanic. I know I would have been upset, had I been him.

And *then* I began researching Red Bluff Airport in preparation for this story. The latest RBL airport-overhead photograph showed nothing but bare ground where the old FBO used to be! A new runway, taxiway, and service apron had bypassed that location altogether.

In a related Red Bluff airport web site, I couldn't help but notice a bold statement which caught my attention: *"The airport is built on an **Indian graveyard** and is believed to be **haunted**."*

So *that* was it! My Cherokee Indian spiritual ancestors had willed my flight into Red Bluff. The flying metal bird was ordained to blast dirt into the offending operator's noisy engine shop. I was merely a ***messenger***, hand-picked by the spirits to torment he-who-dares-conduct-trade over the bones of an American Indian.

That's my story, and I'm stickin' to it!

THERE WILL BE BLOOD!

No bowling alley in this one, though…

In the spring of '85, things were a-buzz at the famous motorcycle Speedway track in San Bernardino. *CHIPs* TV hunk and two-time former World Champion Speedway Star Bruce Penhall would be flying into Inland Motorcycle Speedway [IMS] by helicopter to kick off the annual race named in his honor.

I used to race motorcycles and was a big fan of Penhall's, so I made the suggestion to deliver Bruce in one of our trainers. This would make some money for the company, help promote the sport, and spread the word about our FAA certified training operation – only minutes away by air.

This naturally required an FAA permit for landing an MD 300C at a sporting event, lots of people in the stands, wires and light standards, etc. I produced a detailed sketch of the approach in and out, emergency-landing areas, hazards to flight, and the whole shebang. Not to mention a half dozen phone calls to Norton Air Base, the local Fire Department and Police, certificates of insurance naming every Tom, Dick and Harry as additionally insured, and so forth. "Safety first; nobody gets hurt."

Wednesday was the day of the big race, and the weather was perfect. We had two 300s working that day. Our newest, shiniest 300C was finishing up the last student. I had just signed-off the post-flight inspection of our older trainer, the 300B. I had taken a photographer up for a short photo flight around noon, and the "B" model was apparently done for the day; except for rehearsing the ground handling wheels installation.

The man who volunteered to assist me with the ground handling wheels at the race [GHW] showed up on time to rehearse. "Darv" was a tall, strong man who had once been a city cop. I found him easy to work with, and I appreciated his taking the time to rehearse. There was a step-by-step procedure we needed to follow to speed up the GHW installation and return the track to the racers, safely:

Skids down; Darv and the designated bikini-girl move in; Our VIP deplanes; He does not wave at the crowd until he's well past the blade tips; Darv establishes a safety perimeter under the rotors; 3-minute cool-down of the engine; clutch disengaged; engine off; wait for rotors to stop; Darv moves aft, and pulls down on the tail boom. With the skids angled just-so, I shoot the retaining pin home on the left GWH - over to the right, and done! We move the ship twenty feet and park it. [We did the install/removal twice to make sure Darv had it down.]

Right on schedule, our Training Center Manager reported over the Unicom frequency that my trainer of choice was "on the ground," in plenty of time to detail and refuel before our VIP's limo pulled up to the front door.

An hour passed. The time for Mr. Penhall to be walking through our door was at hand and yet, no cute blond World Champion in sight! Right about then, the phone rang. Penhall's driver was detouring around heavy traffic, asking for alternate directions to the airport - which I gave him, and he hung up.

I looked at my watch again. *Not good!* We were supposed to land *like clockwork* at 20:00 hours, right after the playing of the National Anthem. Racers would be on the starting line, waiting for us to move away from the racing surface. Our static display would sit proudly mid-field during the race. That was the plan, anyway!

Checking the refueling and bubble-cleaning of the 300C, everything was perfect: her seat belts were laid out in straight lines, headsets hanging on the hooks, carpet clean enough to eat off of, etc. And here came Bruce Penhall, only a few minutes late!

No time for a rest stop or long introduction, I accompanied the handsome, compact athlete out to the 300C, got him buckled into the right seat and made a quick job of strapping myself in on the left. Checklist in hand, I made short work of the pre-start procedures, primed the engine and set the throttle *oh-so-carefully.* Then I hit the starter button.

The most *horrible*, metal-grinding sound shot from the starter area of the little four-banger's Lycoming engine, making me stop what I was doing! Mr. Penhall looked at me and I looked at Mr. Penhall. Bruce was no stranger to things mechanical - but not all that familiar with helicopters. He appeared to be reasonably apprehensive, as I'm sure I did!

"That didn't sound very good," I commented over the intercom. Bruce agreed!

"I wonder if it'll do that again?" I questioned, optimistically.

Sure enough, as I pushed the starter button a second time, the horrible shrieking/shredding sound came back – a classic starter-Bendix-unit failure. I mumbled a familiar *expletive* and got on the radio.

Having grounded the primary trainer, I flipped the battery *Master* "off," asked Bruce to follow me, and abandoned ship. We yanked our headsets out of their plugs and made for the backup bird.

Darn the luck, I thought! The backup bird flies okay, but it isn't a shiny showpiece like the *Squawking Goose* we left behind. Going through the start-up list anew, Bruce acted unconcerned with this unusual development - but I wondered to myself, *what else* could go wrong?

With much less drama, the short flight to IMS Speedway went smoothly. I established radio contact with announcer Bruce Flanders, who was keenly aware of our tardy approach. Mr. Flanders assured me our Landing Zone was clear. Racing would be halted until we landed and moved the ship. Banking into our left base leg, we flittered over the motorcycle pit area, turning into the wind for the short dogleg onto the grass infield; smooth as silk!

As Bruce smiled that big, blue-eyed California surfer smile of his, Darv and a pretty young female sauntered up on cue. Mr. Penhall's door was opened and they helped him deplane. Gently closing the door, the trio remembered to duck the main rotors and walked away from the tail rotor. *Thank goodness we rehearsed this*, I thought with satisfaction.

Checking off the Shutdown List: cool-down complete; clutch disengaged; mixture off; engine stop. Battery *Master* off; unbuckle; slip outside as the crowd in the stands gets a good close view of our flying machine, while racers line up for the start - patiently waiting on us.

As I un-stowed the left GHW and waited for the main rotor to finish its last revolution, Darv - unbeknownst to me - prematurely stepped around to the tail area. Bravely dodging the rotating tail feathers, he decided that the main rotors were turning slow enough for him to go ahead and reef down on the tail boom.

As the trainer's skid-toes rocked upward, my *situational awareness* said "uh-oh," and I heard this "***ttthuck!***" back where Darv was. I turned around to the left, wondering *what the heck....?* The crowd saw what happened and let out a collective "*Oooooohhhhh!*"

Darv had pulled the rotating, three-bladed main rotor system down along with the tail boom. The approaching main rotor blade closest to him smote him right between the eyes; hard enough to drive Darv's eyeglasses into the bridge of his nose. As our eyes met, Darv had a look of *chagrin* on his red face, which I forgot about as a trickle of blood ran down his nose, drawing more "Oooohhhhs" from the stands.

Turns out, it was a small cut. Once we finished moving our ship, the track's paramedic stitched Darv up while the noisy races got back under way. Only then could I sigh deeply and Darv couldn't hear me.

TACKLING THE CESSNA 140

Or Anything Else You Can Grab Hold Of

Some aircraft are praised for their cubic capacity or their extraordinary range, some for their raw power. The heroic little airplane in this tale was known for neither, but sometimes just *being there* is important - as a couple of my passengers discovered, one cold, California morning.

Winter in southern California is associated more with swaying palm trees and populated ocean beaches than snow and ice. Then climb in an aircraft and you'll soon discover that the local mountaintops soar as high as windswept 11,503-foot Mt. San Gorgonio. Many others also poke through the clouds, should one be counting mountain bighorn sheep or performing a lofty search and rescue. Hikers do get lost, climbers do get hurt and/or stranded, and someone darned sure has to go get 'em.

Little did I know when I signed on to fly for Western Helicopters, I would be involved in some hairy mountain flying situations with "customers" who were either in big trouble or about to get into big trouble. All these folks briefly had one thing in common: a very unique look in their eyes. Being in my "sixties," I've seen that look before, and the eyes' message is clear: someone has had the bejesus scared out of them!

There comes to mind a certain Cessna 140 pilot who rather mysteriously found himself stationary and "on top of Mt. Baldy" late one January afternoon, in 1983. He had been in contact with Ontario tower moments before and decided to inform them of his unscheduled predicament.

He had ceased being a carefree owner-aviator and by one fashion or another became a pedestrian. Faced with a long walk ahead of him, he removed the aircraft's VHF radio and prepared to leave his treasured tail-dragger behind on the twin-peaked mountaintop. Then the Sheriff showed up in a helicopter to give him a ride. *[We'll get back to the Cessna pilot in a minute.]*

Mt. Baldy has a busy commercial ski operation on its lower southern exposure during the winter months. Hiking to the summit is seasonal, as deep snow and ice often cover the Mt. Baldy trail. Once you get to the top however, the view of southern California and its shoreline on a clear day is spectacular. *[Flying low over the summit - in a light airplane - on a windy day, is not advised.]*

High time mountain helicopter pilot Pete Gillies pointed out to me that the eastern most peak is actually *Mt. San Antonio*, which sports a steel plate documenting its name and 10,064-foot elevation. At the time, I was hovering three feet directly over Mt. San Antonio's metal marker with Pete in the left front seat. The famous Western Helicopter CFI was giving me a thorough mountain-flying refresher course in a pretty white Lama.

Mt. San Antonio's westernmost twin - slightly lower in elevation - bears the Mt. Baldy name, but there's no plaque, Pete informed me. Not far to the southeast is 8,859-foot Mt. Cucamonga, comprising three of the tallest peaks in the area.

We flat-landers read the news of the weird event in the local papers: a Cessna 140 "landing" atop the rounded peak. I recall reading some mention of a performance issue in the pilot's post-incident statement. The airplane boasts a ceiling of 15,500-feet but regardless, the little tail dragger landed where it shouldn't have - with or without power - about 200 feet down the graceful eastern slope of Mt. San Antonio.

However, doing so encroached upon the domain of the San Bernardino County Sheriff and the US Forest Service. The 900-lb airplane would either have to be removed or salvaged where it sat; and quick, for winter storms were on the way!

Pete and I love mountain flying, so we screened incoming calls with interest for anything connected to the Cessna, but nothing. Calls for more mundane jobs were coming in, but with the latest weather forecast, we feared the little airplane was in for a long, cold winter.

A day of cold, wet weather sailed by, and then came the call from a gentleman by the name of "Mel" who wanted to charter our MD500 to take him and a helper to the top of Mt. San Antonio. The Sheriff reported that Mel's Cessna was still there, but that it might have slid down the slope a touch, and was taking on ice.

With another storm predicted to arrive around mid-day, our window of opportunity was small. I was dying to ask Mel exactly how the little plane ended up on Mt. San Antonio, but *no*. What were important were the mission, and the money. If Mel wanted me to know anything else, he'd tell me, I figured.

Mel explained that he wished to be dropped off at the top. He and his helper needed to be left on location for a couple of hours. He was bringing a small assortment of tools with him, the ones required to remove the little bird's ninety-horse Continental C-90 engine from the firewall, before it got enveloped in ice. Mel had enough money for an hour or so of helicopter time, and would be taking advantage of Western's "first-hour-of standby-free" policy.

The very next morning I dispatched our 200-gal Jet-A truck driver to meet me at "Cow Saddle," an unofficial heli-spot for mountain pilots to meet their contacts. "Craig" was an old hand at this game. Taking the map I had marked for him and smiling like a surfer, Craig headed out the door. Both of us knew by the time he navigated the freeways to the Mt. Baldy turn-off, I would be at Cow Saddle, needing fuel.

Looking to the northwest as we climbed out from Rialto's airport, Mel and I got a good look at the darkness heading our way, and tried not to cast doom on our chances of getting the job done. The air was choppy, making the climb to altitude a regular white-knuckler. But we were flying in the vaunted MD500D - *born to tame the mountains* - and like Pete would say, "…the helicopter doesn't know the wind is blowing!"

Establishing a high orbit over Mt. San Antonio, the winds at 11,000-feet were predictable and energetic. Mel took in the sight of his marooned airplane with a sigh I could sense above the noise and turbulence. I wasted little time setting up an approach to the peak and landed with power to spare. The skids sat down on thin ice, which fractured as I lowered the power.

Mel and his helper waited for my signal and deplaned exactly as instructed, offloading their canvas tool bag and securing the seatbelts and doors. They crouched low and made for the left front where they hunkered down and waited for me to lift off.

As I made my way down toward Cow Saddle to standby, I reached Craig on his portable radio. He sounded far away; his signal was barely readable. To make a long story short, I had marked Craig's map with the wrong access road, putting him over twenty miles away to the west! Poor Craig couldn't make head nor tails of his location, or how to find Cow Saddle.

The sky was slowly growing darker and the wind had begun to gust and swirl. I would need fuel before I could fly back for my passengers. Needless to say, I was unhappy with myself for the map error and apologized to Craig when he finally drove up, well over an hour later.

No worries, though: we refueled and I was airborne in time to meet Mel at the arranged pick-up time. Climbing to altitude, I added friction to the cyclic and collective controls to deal with the turbulence. Traversing back and forth up the steep slope, I was soon high enough to see Mel and company again. I observed that they were taking their last few steps toward the hunker-down spot. They looked tired, for some reason.

When I landed, a blind man could have seen the look of sheer exhaustion on the faces of both my passengers. There was Mel's bag of tools at their feet, but I saw no C-90 engine or anything else belonging to the little Cessna. Carefully climbing back in the 500D, Mel's hands were shaking as he slowly buckled in and adjusted his David-Clark's microphone to speak to me. The look in his eyes said it all.

"We slipped on the ice as soon as you took off and we almost died." Mel said, out of breath. With no crampons on their hiking boots, they discovered too late that the "trail" down to the Cessna turned into steep, wet, slippery ice, sending both men sliding out of control down the mountain.

"Our only salvation," Mel gasped between breaths, "was that we both slid within reach of the Cessna's landing gear struts - which we tackled - and held on for dear life!" Bruised and depressed about the little bird's fate, Mel had to break out his tools, hammering foot and hand holes into the numbing ice. They spent the next two hours crawling back up the slope on hands and knees, scared to death.

Aircraft have been left to freeze into the ice all over the planet for over sixty years, but I can assure you that Mel felt terrible about turning his back on his 140. It was time to say goodbye, though. The little tail dragger belongs to the mountain, now.

THE SECRET PROTOCOL OF CUL-DE-SAC SPRING

Either You Know, or You're Toast.

Old timers from the Snake River country near Cottonwood, Idaho could tell you where a special little roadside spring is. It splashes merrily away on the shady side of Graves Canyon Road, almost unseen. All us veteran Idaho heli-loggers, a horde of river-rafters and hundreds of trout fishermen have stopped there and filled up their water jugs for years on end. It's not all that hard to locate, but it helps if you know its secret. Some time ago, a handyman came along and made some ornate brick and mortar improvements around the spring's outlet to elevate the steady stream of water and make the water-gathering experience a little more civilized. Even with improvements, the water only squirted out of a continuous-flow-fixture at a paltry gallon a minute.

The pull-off adjacent to the spring is along a tall fern-covered rock wall on the west side of the broad dirt road. Vehicle parking is always in the shade on a hot afternoon. While a thirsty traveler slowly fills his water bottle, he's got it made; out of the hot sun and happy to see the sparkling water flowing. Happy, unless it was a no-wind day and Graves Canyon Road was bone dry and dusty - as it always got in late summer.

On a hot afternoon during the August drought, you prayed. That's right – prayed, that nobody drove by the spring at their usual forty-miles-an-hour while you were filling up. They'd come flying around the blind corner southbound before you could hear 'em and you were lucky if you got inside your truck and closed the door, otherwise you were screwed - as were your open water jugs: quickly contaminated with talc-like dust.

It would ruin an otherwise perfectly fine *John Muir moment* at the Cul-de-Sac spring, as an inescapable rushing tornado of finely ground talc covered everything, anytime some clown sped by. It seemed like a game to some people. Or maybe they were within their rights, and everybody else should go fill up their danged water jugs in town?

Fast forward to zero nine hundred hours on a warm Friday morning in August, and it is finally pay day for the CRI heli-loggers[11]. We were all told to meet up at the log landing for a pep talk, and then the checks would be handed out. The pay checks arrived two days late, so the word amongst the hookers, cutters, and chasers was, the overhead could go pound sand with their pep talk, because the boys are taking the rest of Friday off. And with that, they jumped back in their assorted dusty rigs and tore off toward Lewiston.

There was not a breeze that early in the morning, and knowing what a bear the road is with all those trucks and cars racing north toward the nearest bank, I kicked back and let the dust settle for a while. Lo and behold, there was Captain Bart, who twelve years from this day would be famous as "The Ax-Men" TV series Huey heli-logging pilot!

Bart was hanging out by the 214B. We crewed the 214B together, but with the loggers all mad and gone to town, we suddenly had the day off. It looked like Bart was having a ball, though, rubbing the tail rotor clean with a roll of blue shop towels. Bart used to fly choppers in the Navy, so I figure him being an officer and all, he was somehow deprived of getting dirty all those years and he's making up for it now, rubbing up against grody civilian helicopters on his time off.

Me, not so much. But the heavy dust over the road had finally settled, so I bid Bart adieu and made my way back to the junky old Suburban. The loggers called the rig I was borrowing that morning a "crummy," owing to its odor, perhaps - and near-dead mechanical condition. Loading up a couple of Bart's water jugs and two of my own, I headed slowly up the road toward the spring.

It was getting hot by then, and I was starting to perspire a little. The pull-off wasn't far up ahead, and if I was living right, there'd be no road traffic while I watered up. Easing over to the left, I put 'er in "P," got all the jugs out and began the slow filling process. I had half of them filled

---

[11] Chet Raspberry Inc., whose logging division was managed by Brian Burr at that date in time.

with cold water when I heard another vehicle coming from the direction of the log landing.

It was "Snake," one of our CRI hookers, no less - driving another CRI crummy. He drove up slow enough that I didn't get caked with dirt as he pulled into the shade, a couple of spaces behind my rig. It turns out, Snake had been having a powwow with the Woods Boss after the checks were handed out and missed the earlier stampede into town.

Sliding off his car seat, the husky logger dragged some canteens and plastic jugs along with him, looking amused about something. When our eyes met, he said, "Hey, Captain, how's the water flowin'?" "Cold and clean, Snake!" I replied, screwing the top down on the last jug. I set my containers off to one side as Snake began the water-filling process.

Turns out Snake's crummy and mine had some things in common. As he patiently filled his containers, he repeated the key points of a conversation he had just had with the Woods Boss, how the company needed to get both crummys' radiators flushed out, and some new mud and snow tires, to get 'em ready for winter. They ran okay, he agreed. Both Suburbans had big healthy V-8s with automatic transmissions, but they sounded like hot rods from too many holes in their mufflers. "Need to get that fixed, too."

I had one last water jug to load in the crummy when Snake brought up another problem common to both rigs – half of our electric windows won't motor up or down! Screwing the lid down tight on his last jar, Snake frowned a little and went on in his rambling manner, saying, "We need to get 'em fixed, due to the cold and dust…."

Snake halted in mid-sentence, looking sort of sideways at me. Dressed like a raggedy pirate, Snake was heavily tattooed, had a mouth full of bad teeth and a black do-rag on his head that was beginning to spot with sweat. He had left his driver's door wide open and his engine idling on purpose.

As soon as he said "*dust*," the lights came on, and he realized that I was standing closer to my rig than he was to his. Although my engine was switched off, the driver's side door was open, and my cargo was already loaded up. The Captain's crummy was a full car length ahead of Snake's, and the Captain had that shit-eating Okie grin on his face.

Snake realized suddenly that I knew the secret protocol of the spring, which was to take off like ***a bat out of hell*** while the other sucker was still climbing into his rig. The idea was to be the lead rig and drive like a maniac the last two miles to the highway - leaving the other clown in your choking dust. Snake grabbed his containers and lit off like *the dentist* was after him.

Okies catch on quick to the lame-brained mind games loggers love to play, as Snake was about to find out. Oh, he made it interesting by *flying* to his rig like a greasy streak of lightning, flinging his water jugs wildly through the open window, and leaping into the driver's seat.

With the ignition "on" and my driver's side door wide open, I sucked my landing gear inside, cranked the gear selector lever down to "1" and floored it. My Suburban's mud-and-snow tires spun and spewed insanely, scattering unspeakable nastiness behind me as my door slammed shut and I rocketed forward, fishtailing like a Great White.

The pirate's rig roared to life behind me like an infuriated top-fuel dragster, bringing him almost alongside - about my eight o'clock position - and holding steady as both of us adrenaline surfers committed ourselves to an all-out drag race.

Naturally, I wouldn't be writing this story if I had *lost*. And I probably shouldn't have gotten such righteous satisfaction out of "dusting" my old hookin' buddy - as my bucket of bolts pulled steadily ahead of his - filling Snake's ventilated vessel with clouds of hideous dirt, to the point he had to shut 'er down and pull the heck over.

HAVE LAMA, WILL TRAILER

And the More Pickup You've Got, the Better.

The microwave antennae lift in downtown San Francisco was rained out before we got the last two dishes up. You'd think we could have hung two more of the cornucopia-shaped gizmos in the rain - just to be done with all the incredible red tape it took to get there, but no. It was raining in earnest. Sparks were shooting from the steel climbers' boots and bonding wires, and my saturated leather jacket was heavy with rain, threatening to pull me out the Lama's open right-hand door with its ungainly mass.

Postponement of the job was a major pain, but we were flying for a very big customer in the telecommunications game, so we rolled with the punch. The SA-315B Lama on loan to me had to be trailered back to Utah, but I'd get another one coming this way as soon as the weatherman gave us a decent window. Whatever it took to do the job, we did it.

A second "low pressure" system was far out to sea but imminent. All our special permits were hanging on a clear window after the storm. Banking on an accurate weather report, I rescheduled for the early morning hours, right after storm passage.

At dawn on the morning of the big lift, I suddenly felt like singer, Tony Bennett. Facing west from the 44th floor's outdoor observation deck, the bejeweled Pacific Ocean lay spread-eagled for all of San Francisco to gloat upon. Seabirds celebrated the arrival of the sun while steaming ghosts rose lazily from manholes in Market Street, far below. There was not the slightest breeze; the entire storm's energy had headed for Reno. Perfect!

Hanging the last two dishes on top of the sky scraper was almost an anti-climax, having lifted off from the trailer and hovered straight up, 900 feet. Seeing the expressions on the faces of the random secretary/office-worker going by was priceless, as I flew straight up and straight down to Number One Market Street's safety barricade.

Invariably on the way up, random observers would freeze in their tracks, gasping. As they stared from the sterility of their offices' steel-and-glass environment, my colorful 36-foot wide, three-bladed French rotor-system appeared, lifting my wasp-shaped helicopter straight up. Not to mention the grinning pilot and that strange-looking, high-tech fiberglass antenna dangling far below him. All too quickly, the job was done.

The SFO job depended upon rolling the Lama in and out of the prestigious location on a custom-built helicopter trailer. Landing back on the trailer after such an adrenaline rush was a bit trickier than the take-off, but before you could say *Ghirardelli Square*, the Lama's skids were locked down tight and its red and yellow main rotor blades stored in their padded container for Phase Two: a long road trip to Arizona, where scores of tall wooden "telephone poles" were being framed with cross-arms. A new 69KV power line through the rolling Arizona foothills was ready to go vertical, as soon as the Lama and I got there.

There were a couple of things I liked about "621," the white 1980 Chevrolet pickup truck assigned to me for this trip. One was the "fifth wheel" towing set-up, which made pulling the long, 2300-lb helicopter (facing backwards) child's play. It was much better than the old bumper-hitch set-up.

The other thing I liked about Chevy's three-quarter ton pickup was that big block, 454 CID[12] V8 engine under the hood. It came with a huge four-barrel carburetor and I didn't have to pay for the gas, which meant if one truly mashed on the gas pedal, one instantly felt powerful acceleration - while the heavily muffled, single-pipe-exhaust system made all those horses sound more like one bloated old cow: "MOOOOOOOOO!"

It's a long haul from SFO to Bakersfield, my next proposed fuel stop. If you've driven Interstate 5 as many times as I have, you know it can be terribly straight and boring. The bare-market AM radio mounted in the truck's dash did little to keep me entertained. That's probably why I gave the hitchhiker a second glance, as I pulled out of the busy truck stop with a full tank of gas.

He looked down on his luck but harmless enough. Guess I thought maybe he'd be musically inclined, play a harmonica expertly and keep me singin' until we got to Bakersfield, ignoring the unwritten company policy of not picking up hitchhikers, I pulled over onto the shoulder. The

---

[12] 7.4 liter Gas Guzzler.

young man's face lit up as I did so, you could almost read his thoughts "…a chopper on a trailer is giving me a ride!"

He came running up to the door with a day pack and was soon inside, thanking me for stopping 'cause he'd been standing there a long time 'cause the s.o.b. who gave him a ride this far took off suddenly and left him standing there and now he's all excited about the helicopter, saying he was going to jump on the trailer whether I stopped or not cause he was good at stuff like that and asked "Can you fly it?" and he's really looking forward to getting to LA but he doesn't have any friends there, so he might have to hit somebody up for some money and try to hang out in Hollywood for a couple of days, and then he's headin' east to Texas, back to some rinky-dink one-horse town where he got throwed in jail a few months back, got caught doing "something," but then he got out and had to leave Texas long enough for them to forget about him so he could come right back a few months later and show them dumb cops he can't be told what to do nor where to do it!

Long before my big ears verified my mistake, my Okie nose realized I had erred in giving this little degenerate a ride before he started talking. The kid packed around with him his own special odor. Not that *basketball-player-in-the-fourth-quarter* aroma. More like an old logging *crummy*[13] smells after a few wet winters of hard use, where scores of old lunch sacks, half-full of rotten remnants lie forever in dank, dark recesses between the cushions and underneath the seats.

"Stinky" gave off similar obnoxious fumes, something between *bad buttermilk* and *fresh baby diaper*. I opened the driver's side vent window wide open and drove faster.

It was suddenly a longer leg under these new conditions. I got busy mentally, trying to come up with a rescue plan for yours truly. My eyes were beginning to water like the time I flew that seismic survey in northern California. It was raining back then. I had to fly the surveyor and his helpers all over the place in an MD500D with all the doors on tight. "The Creosote Kid" always sat next to me in the center seat, because he was slender.

Every time we landed, the Creosote Kid took off with his Mini-Mac chain saw, running through the head-high sage and creosote bushes,

---

[13] Usually and old dilapidated Chevrolet Suburban with seating for eight passengers

cutting a straight line for the surveyor. The Kid apparently **never** washed his work clothes, so after a month or so, the saw-gas and creosote stench on this guy was *killer*. It finally got so bad I told him to go wash his &$#@! clothes or I wouldn't let him fly with me anymore.

The Kid took it kinda hard. I felt like I may have shot a "team player" for a moment. Then half of the other seismic hands came around to thank me, because the Kid was killing them too, but they didn't want to be the first admit it. Such is the curse of my finely tuned Oklahoma nose.

Now here I am, stuck with *Bad Buttermilk* and no harmonica. It was a long way down Interstate 5 before I would have a decent place to pull over and let my passenger go stink up someone else's truck. And he never shuts the heck up, it would appear.

Two arduous hours later, I pulled off the Interstate in Bakersfield. I parted ways with Stinky, but not before he mooched a hot meal off me at the busy truck-stop café. I didn't worry about the money; it was well spent, just to be rid of him. I could have driven on through Los Angeles, but no.

My timely detour would take me east on Highway 58 through Tehachapi, while Stinky hoped to continue on his smelly way to L.A. He grabbed his pack and sauntered off, glancing back over his shoulder as he did so. There was no way he was getting back in my truck. And I made sure he wasn't sitting in the Lama's cockpit or standing anywhere near the trailer when I pulled out of the dusty truck terminal!

I explained to Stinky that I had to head to Mojave and points east, so our paths had naturally come to a fork. Later in the evening, I pulled over to check in with Operations. Word was that the customer in Arizona had called to delay my arrival by two days, giving me time to drive the hundred-miles or so home and enjoy the time off.

Exactly two days later, I am heading east from Rialto on Interstate 10. The power line job was a "go" once again and I was fueled up for the first long leg: Rialto to Quartzsite, Arizona. Although my refueling point was way out in the middle of nowhere, I knew of a good truck stop with an easy way of getting back on the freeway. Been there before.

Crossing over the Interstate Bridge, the I-10 east onramp invited me to turn left. As I did so, a familiar-looking transient stood there with his thumb out, and that silly look was back on his face. *Buttermilk!* He grabbed his pack, gave me a shout and ran toward the Lama. I gave 621 both spurs and lots of rein, and she said, MOOOOOOOOOOOOO!!

THE BIG SHIPMENT

a.k.a. The ol' Manchurian End-Around

By the time this maverick's left-seat résumé became a three pager, I had the pleasure of working for one of the largest helicopter operators in North America, three or four medium-sized operators and even a single-ship operator. One thing all these "operators" had in common: they had to bust their butts to pay the astronomical bills that came 'round in the mail. *"Cash is King! Keep the machines flying! Bring in outside business!"* was the word shouted down to the masses.

At our mid-sized California helicopter base, we felt the heat. One customer needed a simple 206B-paint job, another needed a stereo installed in his 369HE, and there was the random flight instruction student. But the rotor blades of commerce weren't turning fast enough and there was nothing substantial on the horizon to calm the nerves of the Overhead, so the rest of us searched high and low for elusive *opportunity*.

And then it happened: one of our wily entrepreneurs came up with an *ingenious* way to make money in our spacious hangar, without turning a blade!

"The Big Shipment," as explained by the Boss, involved the partial disassembly and re-packaging of scores of brand new Hughes 500E helicopters, fresh off the California assembly line. A wealthy customer in Germany was said to be impatiently awaiting their arrival. Although we were a qualified Hughes Service Center, no one had ever done anything on a scale like this - but that didn't stop us from taking on the work.

A long row of new Hughes 500s in various modern paint schemes soon stretched from the big hangar way out to the north ramp, and white tractor-trailers were pulling into the yard with more. We carefully hoisted them off the trucks one by one, slapped on a set of ground-handling-wheels and rolled them into the hangar for packaging.

It was quite a procedure to drain the fuel, package-up the rotor blades, tail feathers, rotor heads and masts; remove the tail boom and skid gear; box up the drive shafts and other components securely in custom made wooden crates - and levitate the fuselage and all the pieces into the first of many empty "conex" oversea containers - which were also arriving on flatbed trailers.

The project had sounded fairly simple – to hear our Boss say it - but we ran into a sticky little problem right off the bat: getting the landing gear shock struts compressed far enough to remove them turned out to be a knuckle-busting nightmare! But we found two feisty A&Ps who could do it faster than anyone, and kept them focused on that job.

Pilot-types like me stayed busy fabricating special wooden brackets on band saws and drill presses to hold various disassembled parts securely in their applicable boxes. Once the fuselage was secured to a wooden cradle, hundreds of fingerprints had to be wiped from the paint, while the plastic had to be Mirror Glazed spotlessly clean, inside and out. With eight to ten people working like harmonious bees, we eventually had four disassembled helicopters cleverly wedged into one conex container, a large steel box that was expected to accommodate <u>five</u> helicopters!

After a bit of head-scratching, a number of phone calls to the factory and pencil sketches made within a rectangle to grok the problem, everything was carefully off-loaded from the conex. Plan B's arrangement was adapted, allowing our fifth flying machine to be squeezed into the last wedge of empty space - just barely. Locking the bar down over the twin, hinged-steel doors, our party of ten breathed a sigh of relief, amid a sea of soda cans and pizza boxes.

Yes, fellow helophiles, by the time the first conex full of immaculate helicopters was backed onto a tractor-trailer and sent sailing for the Panama Canal, we had the *how-to-do-it* down pat. Some of the crew were nursing cuts and bruises from bucking the fussy shock-struts, exposure to keen metal edges, fragile drain lines and sharp wooden splinters - but our gung-ho group pitched in and went to work on the next ship in line.

In the midst of all this good, clean, American enterprise, I paused to take pride in our closely-knit crew for their collective enthusiasm and lack of interest in the time clock. Before we knew it, our talented gang had tackled the yard full of 500s, under budget and on time. Accounting's impressive invoice was faxed, a lot of money changed hands, and another payroll deadline was met.

Smug from our accomplishments and hungry to do more of this wonderful work, you can't possibly fathom the disdain and disbelief we all felt when – a few months later - someone in a dark suit from the State Department informed our Boss that all those flying machines had found a not-so-happy-home……in North Korea!

Ouch. Just thinking about it makes me "ill!"

PILOT IN A PAINTER'S PARADOX

A Brush with Fate!

Somewhere between the cities of Colton and Riverside, California, an aluminum-colored steel bridge erupts out of the ground to suspend a hefty gas pipeline over a wide, sandy river. The long, graceful structure spans the Santa Ana riverbed in a splendid arch from the north bank to the south bank. You might not notice it driving by; tall trees abound and few roads access the gas company's right of way. I got to know the bridge a little too well on a sunny day in 1991.

o o o o o

Hiser Helicopter's Chief Pilot, Bill Ferguson, put his potential customer on "hold" and gestured to the Director of Operations sitting across the desk from him. That would be me. The former Korean War F-86 Sabre jet fighter pilot sitting five feet south of me had an amused look on his weathered face, making his gray, handlebar moustache spread its hairy wings. Leaning back in his creaky office chair, he propped two fine ostrich-skin boots up on the corner of his tidy desk.

"*The Colonel*," as we called him, was smiling about *Wacky Caller Number 489*, code words we used when fielding a phone call from anyone who wanted to do something *wacky* with one of Floyd Hiser's helicopters. *Lo and Behold*, the caller was a legitimate paint contractor, inquiring if we could hover over the structure in mention while his son painted the hard-to-reach stretches?

The contractor explained that he had already painted the underside of the bridge the hard way, using long ladders. An hour or so in a chopper should be enough, he speculated. I raised my eyebrows just *so*, nodded for Bill's amusement, and let the contractor's request sink in. Although

I'd never done any *aerial painting*, my job was to open the door when opportunity knocked.

Sensing this was something the Boss might approve of, I quoted "Mike" a set-up fee that had some *fat* on it, plus a handsome hourly flight rate for our MD 500D. That didn't scare him off. He had the cash. That was why our Chief Pilot was smiling so. He won't have to do the flying!

Digging for more details, I took down Mike's information and performed a job recon. Sure enough, the chalky, steel bridge appeared to be a treacherous perch for anyone trying to stand on it - much less carry any equipment. The 500D was no threat to the gas line, worst-case scenario.

The contractor was betting that his painter - wielding a heavy-duty roller on an extension pole - could work from the 500D's right cargo basket, carrying five gallons of paint around with him. A "Dave Busse-approved" photographer's harness was available to enhance his son's safety.

I saw no other way to get it done, and documented my findings in an application relative to the close-by Riverside Airport, and the usual fire agencies. A modicum of red tape was involved.

Joining us on the flight line to check out our 500D two days later, contractor Mike introduced us to his son, "Robin," the designated painter. They brought along the equipment Robin would be using. Dressed in coveralls, thick knee pads, painter's gloves, and our lightweight David Clark hard-hat with eye shield, Robin demonstrated he could kneel in the basket and apply paint well below skid level. A metal grate above the bucket would allow him to roll off any excess paint.

Our next immediate concern was keeping our 500D's paint job from being spoiled in the process. The product Mike needed to apply was thick, industrial strength aluminum paint, designed to stick to metal and stay there for years. Mike assured us he would have the required paint solvent and enough rags on hand for that purpose.

Our four-way safety harness was fully adjustable, allowing Robin plenty of mobility. He would have some peace of mind knowing I could visually and aurally monitor his activities as I piloted from the left front seat. And if Robin were to stumble from the cargo basket for any reason, a man-safe strap attached to the helicopter's upper steel hard-point would arrest his fall.

We addressed the usual safety concerns about doing low-level work of the hazardous variety, including loose objects and anyone accidentally introducing paint rollers into the rotor blades. But neither was deterred, saying that the bridge simply had to be finalized. They were eager to proceed and paid half of the total estimate, motivating me to draw up a plan.

There was little drama following our formal application, which was express-mailed to the Federal Aviation Administration. After the standard business week, Hiser's copy came back stamped *approved* with nary a hiccough. The insurance companies approved, too. As *Paint Day* neared, the weatherman came through.

The cool November morning dawned sunny and winds were not a factor. The job was only a few minutes by air from Hiser base, and we had a grassy landing zone near the bridge. Fuel Boss Tom Burgess arrived first, hung two wind streamers up, and monitored his VHF portable. We shut down after landing and had a safety briefing before stirring the paint and strapping it on.

Stationing Tom's Jet-A tanker near the north end of the bridge, he and Mike stood by to load more paint into the bucket, clean off any splatter on the ship, and refuel the 500D as needed. Tom also had two 20-pound fire extinguishers, which I prayed we wouldn't need.

It was predictable Robin would need paint more often than I would need fuel, so we filled the ship only halfway to keep hover-power and flight-control muscle-demands to a minimum. No hydraulics on our little workhorse. After an hour or so of hover-work, pilot fatigue was a reality.

Hovering about a foot above the bridge, Robin started painting everything he could reach. This was his first helicopter ride, and he was having a ball. We were able to chat over the intercom's "hot mike" feature when he needed me to move in any certain direction. Our 500D was Burl Yehnert's first "E Model" nose job. So doors off, I could observe Robin with peripheral vision.

Robin proved to be a strong lad and was able to work fast, all hunched over. He used long, two-fisted strokes to paint to the upper steel surfaces. Loading up his hairy roller frequently, he would briefly sit upright on his knees - scrub off any excess paint - then bend back over the side of the basket and get to work. He rested only when his paint ran low - then back to the landing zone.

We kept ahead of the errant paint that flipped onto the skids, the basket and elsewhere - although it took some *elbow grease* to loosen any hardened blobs. Loading up the paint can one last time, we took off with 250 pounds of Jet-A to finish our metal masterpiece.

The job was actually going about as Mike envisioned; we could see the end in sight. The south "X-Bar" [tension equalizer] was painted, ditto the north "X-Bar." Robin the *Wonder Boy* only needed to apply a generous coat to this thing called the "knuckle," and it would be **Miller Time.**

Glancing up momentarily from my hazardous hover, I noticed Tom had his binoculars out. He was watching us work while another employee shot videos. Tom normally sang happy western melodies at work; but he was nervous today - I could tell. To point out how needless it was to worry about us, I went and got my skids stuck inside the bridge as Robin was painting away.

I didn't mean to get stuck. Our center of gravity (CG) changed at a bad time. Robin kept saying, "… *a little more to the right. Now go down a little, and forward.*" In leaning out of the basket, the young painter shifted our CG laterally to the right, as my skids fed back bumps and thumps.

My left skid's toe was rubbing a horizontal steel member crossing underneath us, but the right skid toe was underneath the sloping member. When I eased the ship forward, the right rear skid-heel slipped off a parallel member just behind us - dropping us down inside a tubular steel cage, inches above that high-pressure gas line. Uh-oh. The tail rotor was in the clear, at least.

Now I had hardly any forward or lateral movement; metal to metal contact on each corner. It didn't take *nervous Tom* long to kibitz over the radio, "*Dorcey, your skids are stuck!*" Robin glanced my way as if asking, *Now what?* Like any good lift pilot would, I eased off pressure on the controls, allowing the ship to bobble while I consulted the Operators Manual for a remedy.

Well, not really. But to reverse our CG problem, I had *Wonder Boy* sit straight up and lean against the airframe. Sure enough, with a little jiggling of the cyclic, collective and tail-feathers we rose up and away - like a bug floating out of one's ear. Collectively, we started breathing again, savoring the breeze as we buzzed back over to the landing zone, after our brush with fate.

THE ONE-HANDED MECHANIC

Not by handicap, but by choice.

This happened on one of those heli-logging jobs in Paradise, and I kid you not, most of the crew and I were camped out at the Paradise RV Park, right in the middle of Paradise Valley. Montana loggin' in the spring is hard to beat, and it says so, right there on the map!

Of course, "spring" is in March, and there's plenty of nasty weather blowin' out of Canada now and then all the way through May. But mostly it's where you wish you could camp out cheap and work hard year 'round. Or until the unmentionable hits the fan, as it did for one of my favorite one-handed mechanics.

Fred did not appear to have any physical handicaps when we first met. Six feet tall, dark and stout, Fred was a good lookin' young A&P Mechanic. A decade or two younger than this Huey loggin-pilot, but I'd heard from around town that he could truly crew a Huey. I've seen able-bodied men humbled by the task, but it was my job to fly logs and somebody else would have to pass judgment on Fred; unless, of course, he fell short of his responsibilities, somehow.

One of those responsibilities was keeping-up our little corner of a farmer's meadow where the boss had negotiated a sweet deal for our Huey's Service Landing Zone. The entrance to the LZ was near the highway. It was gated, and all around us was nothing but forty acres of fenced, flat pastureland for grazing. A bucolic paradise, at that. Our crafty mobile maintenance unit was already parked level, in the shade of the big tree. In the midst of the LZ sat the pride of the fleet, the ghostly white *Lorena*.

Lorena earned her keep by flying heavy logs all day long, as fast as we could latch on to them and drop them off at the log landing. At the end of a hard day, flying back to the sunny meadow was always a spiritual event for me, as my bod tingled from hours of bustin' my hump; but I loved it!

I especially loved shutting off all the noise and savoring the sudden silence as I signed my name to records of import. As the Lycoming turbine and composite rotor blades hissed to a stop, I could begin to hear Fred talking under the sputtering of the idling gas truck.

Unstuck finally from the cruel metal seat, I climbed out; more like *poured* out onto the skid's flat toe, then another small step for man, down to the cool green grass with the left Nike and into the fragrant, green cow pie with the right. Sweet.

During all this, my trusty one-handed mechanic has begun his hours-long ordeal of wrenching on, wiping down and refueling *Lorena*. With the main rotor fore-and-aft, our mid-sized service tanker sits ten feet away from the noble UH-1H, the PTO delivering a nice steady flow of Jet-A to the ship's center fuel tank.

A power generator throbs over by the maintenance trailer, powering battery chargers and florescent lights, as well as loud, portable stereo units. *Miss Nibbles* - Fred's ever-present dog - is at my feet sniffing everything and barking loudly at everyone who comes around to *her* LZ. Jack Russells are like that. [Sniff that right shoe all you like, dog.]

I knew it would take Fred longer to do all he had to do, because I seldom recall seeing him without one arm or the other tied up holding on to that precious telephone of his, linked so dependably to an unhappy woman on the West Coast.

Walking his way slowly around the tail section for a general post-flight of the big pieces, Fred was simultaneously talking all "hang-dog" to his far-away wife, with one hand tightly clenched around the cell phone, apparently welded to his left ear.

Fred will never hear the last word about *anything*, from what I briefly overheard-much less how to do all his many chores while he's being ranted at. "One more week, honey, I'll be home to fix it then. I'll take the kids campin', I promise. One more week, now remember what we talked about, honey. Aww, come on, now."

Sliding at last into my comfortable ride, my butt feels practically electric and I am ready for the short ride to a Hot Shower in Paradise; but there I go again. [You gotta jump on them metaphors with both Nikes!]

And then came the peculiar large yellow patch in the middle of our previously green LZ. Fred had gone on break by then but there was another sign pointing in his direction: we were short one hundred and fifty gallons of go-juice! The fuel had made it as far as the truck, but careful record keeping showed it had been pumped out.

Yep, you guessed it. Lost in the sound of the generators, barking dogs, and an incessant noise in one ear, Fred had forgotten that he was pumping fuel. Easing up on his professional routine, he allowed himself to be distracted and unwittingly created an ecological disaster that required substantial mitigation. And a new employer for Fred - someplace *far* from Paradise!

FLIGHT OF THE ENGINEER

"Some policies were meant to be bent," says he.

Right around August, after the turn of the twenty-first century, fire season hit the Cascade Mountains of the northwestern USA and yours truly went from his comfy Idaho-based Huey-logging operation to Call-When-Needed-Restricted-Cat. Helicopter, Type II – Medium. *Have Bambi Bucket, will travel.* [Hold my mail, Momma, here I go again.]

I'm used to the routine, as I cut my teeth fighting fires right out of the Army. Been there, and so on. Lots of fire camp T-shirts in my collection. Was actually hoping my current logging operation would keep me engaged in Huey-logging, though. The disparity in pay between log-jockey and firefighter did not sit well with Lourdes, the lady for whom I live and breathe. She telephoned from high atop our stack of bills: *"Keep loggin', Weeengo!"* and rang off.

Twenty days later I am standing on the apron of a fine little north-south airstrip along Interstate 5 in southwestern Oregon, where our loggin'-Huey-turned-firefighter has come to rest after a protracted skirmish with the local conflagration. Having been freshly released by Fire Dispatch, I awaited the arrival of another Huey pilot who was en route via our employer's Cessna. My relief jockey would fly our tricked-out Huey to another fire, while I met up with *my favorite mechanic* - a gentleman we shall know as "Jim" - at the aforementioned airstrip, around noon.

They grow 'em big up in Canada, and Jim was no exception. Big and tall, red-headed and blue eyed, he was. And "lucky" I was to be traveling with Jim; like a dog was "lucky" to have fleas, and you'll know why, soon enough!

When the fires broke, Jim and I had to drop everything and leave our cozy campers near the Salmon River in northeastern Idaho. Afterward, the Big Cheese in Operations decreed that Jim and yours truly should jump in the Cessna (a nice little 206) and his Part 91 pilot would fly us nonstop from Roseville, OR to Salmon, ID that very afternoon. Then we could both go on break!

[Somebody had *warned* me about Jim a year or so beforehand. The pilot was just passing on a little "care and feeding" information about a certain mechanic, something that a friend would want another friend to know. Common courtesy, and I'll wager mechanics singled out the prima donna pilots, too. The thing was, Jim was licensed in the USA as an "A&P mechanic" but coming from Canada, mechanics are referred to as "engineers," ergo more in charge and better educated than the given stateside mechanic.

Let me assure you I had no problem with the man's credentials or his skills; far from it. It was only Jim's attitude I objected to, one that sported a built-in camber and was slightly over-torqued. But that's okay, I've learned to walk the razor's edge over the years; Jim is the *Engineer*. We'll do it *Jim's* way, and *oh yes*, we're going to totally overlook the fact that Jim has once again brought his *wonderful* **dog** along with him, in flagrant violation of the Company's "**No Dogs**" Policy.

"Fluffy" was as cute as any odiferous, long-haired dog could be in a hot, cramped airplane in August, and due to the weight and bulk of his steel travel cage, water dish and *hearty-chow* dog food, Jim was *forced* to leave two of his valuable tool boxes behind. They would be dealt with later by a non-engineer.

The Cessna pilot and I exchanged multiple glances as Jim tried first one way and then the other to fit his well-fed dog's cage into the hold along with all our stuff, maneuvering the pet door so he could tend to the animal as we crossed over some serious mountains on the long, hot flight ahead.

I admired the Cessna pilot's professionalism as he dealt with the Engineer's unnecessary turmoil and setbacks in stride. We finally locked Jim and Fluffy away in the rear of the plane and I jumped in the right front seat to help navigate and look for traffic.

Up front was also as far away as we could get from our four-legged friend, who tensed up visibly when our tardy pilot poured the coals to the howling six-banger up front. The pooch went ***poo poo poo*** climbing up and over the Cascades. Undaunted, our pilot wasn't turning back over that. We peered past the propeller with purpose. "East by southeast, pilot!"

Our polite pilot and I came to admire the thoughtful wind-vents that Cessna provides front-seaters in this model. Fresh, cool air screamed into the cockpit - mixing with the tepid, fouled atmosphere Fluffy and the Engineer were sharing in the back.

Climbing to eleven thousand, five hundred feet, we really didn't require verbal confirmation as to what the gaseous canine was doing, for Jim and beast whined a pitiful duet. Jim may have worked on aircraft, but clearly he was no flyer! That went double for his dog. Jim would have paid a king's ransom for a fresh air vent about then, but **no**. *Pilots* in *front, Engineers and* pressurized *dogs* in *back*, and no changing seats in flight. Ain't no way, pal.

Onward over the Ochocos to the Malheur we pooed, wallowing over the Wallowa-Whitmans and bounding down the bouncy backside of the Salmons, where our cloud-hopper got into some honest-to-goodness, strap-'em-down-tight turbulence! That's when the *real* moaning began in the back.

Was the Frank Church-River-of-No-Return-Wilderness upsetting the Engineer, we wondered? Perhaps *The Church* just didn't stand up visually to the majestic *Canadian Rockies*? No, that wasn't the issue, for Jim whipped out a hefty Zip-Lock bag and dived between his kneecaps.

A lengthy, vocally orchestrated case of the North American *dry heaves* emanated from the Engineer thereafter, until wheels-down.

Salmon Airport seemed an awfully long way to fly under such circumstances, but I'm proud to report that the courageous Cessna pilot and I cowboy'd up, throughout. We were delighted, nonetheless, to open the breezy side windows upon rollout, step out of the fragrant fixed-wing into the cedar scented valley and admire the dramatically beautiful Bitterroot Mountain Range.

Fluffy was obviously relieved. Several minutes elapsed before Jim sat upright and slowly got to his feet.

Legends, like nicknames, come and go in the Wild West. Some talk the talk, some walk the walk. As for Fluffy and the Engineer, I hear they are no longer flying together.

That's Big Jim's policy, now!

STATIC ELECTRICITY AND GOING FETAL

Helicopter Lightning, Phase Two

The Captain's last mention of *helicopter lightning* took place under a hovering Huey and you may recall that it shocked the heck out of four mountain-climbing Nevada concrete workers. After a brief recess to screw up their courage, they gathered bonding wires anew to guide the static electricity to ground. We then resumed the manly task at hand.

Not long after, yours truly transmogrified himself into a Huey logging pilot. Flying over snow-covered logs all day became a love affair with gravity, dancing with Mother Nature every now and then to get our butts kicked.

One gets pretty good with a long-line and remote hook after many years of practice-practice-practice. Good enough to cleverly avoid touching green tree limbs that come between the Captain and the *hooker* far below. *Branches absorb the charge from the hook, and we'll have none of that*, the Captain conspired silently. The unsuspecting hooker reaches up with a gloved hand, not aware that the remote hook is *hot*.

Okay, this is actually a *game* that manly heli-loggers play off and on, to amuse themselves. Everybody gets shocked now and then, it is truly inevitable. On a good day, the hook has barely enough *pop* to make one notice. Unless, of course, one is standing in water or one's boots are wet. Then it'll get your attention.

But on a *bad day* - which looks like any other day – the hooker either does a 100-meter dash or ends up on the ground in what is referred to as the *fetal position*. As dark, flat-bottomed clouds gather in the sky, who would notice? The hookers are too busy ropin' logs - and of course

- nobody but a rookie is going to announce over the radio that the hook is *hot*. That takes all the *fun* out of it!

"*Cowboy*" comes to mind, and a heck of a conventional logger he was. He signed on when we were heli-logging up near Libby, Montana. He was good-natured and had a white hard hat with a Stetson shape to it, ergo the nickname. He'd run like a mad man and holler "*Hawww!*" when he was clear. I'd laugh and fly his logs to the landing.

Several days of this mind-numbing activity went by with fair weather. The ground was dry and the Captain was growing bored as the fifth cycle ground along. *One more log-truck load and we'll be off like a prom dress*, I mulled.

Taking "Jeffro's" last turn, I heard a distinct "***pop***" in my helmet's earphones and observed Jeffro doing an animated dance 200-feet below - but making no after-shock-radio-commentary. *Hmmm*, the Captain deduced. The hook is *hot!*

Now why go and spoil Jeff's fun by telling Cowboy that the hook is hot, when Cowboy can find out for himself, both Jeff and I silently conspired. As the Huey's heavy remote hook cleared the last branch between us by inches, Cowboy extended his pink hand and Lo and Behold, the legendary blue spark from hell leapt from the hook and into Cowboy. Who dropped to the ground and shriveled into the classic fetal position.

To his credit, Cowboy *had* simultaneously crammed a choker eye into the remote hook.

I casually radioed "*Hooker down*," while safely maneuvering Cowboy's one log "pumpkin" off to the log deck.

"*You did that on purpose*," Cowboy whined, as I flew away. Jeffro was on his radio fast, laughing his head off for setting up the rookie heli-logger. "*Ha-haaaaaa!*" he chided *Cowboy-in-the-dirt*. "Oh by the way, everyone," Jeff howled, "…the hook is **HOT!**"

That was almost as memorable as the Hignite heli-drill job I worked near Richfield, Utah. This was back when the seismic core-drills were powered by Dodge 360-CID V8 engines and each "move" was composed of four or five "picks." We were flying Lamas then.

As those familiar flat-bottomed cumulus clouds gathered slowly in the sky, I brought the heavy "skid" base unit within reach. Two of the strongest looking guys on the mountain grabbed the half-ton rig like it was a toy and bossed it into position. Working shirtless, they looked like buff gladiators down below, shiny with sweat and determined to set-up the last drill for the day, come hell or....

The compressor came last, the heaviest piece. It took all my Lama had to hover out of ground effect over the skid and hold it stationary while one of the two muscle-bound men reached out to steady the heavy steel unit. He was four feet away when *the blue bolt from hell* suddenly filled the space between his fingers and the nasty compressor.

Gladiator "A" is now doing the advertised 100-meter dash uphill, blowing past the other gladiator, who has seen the messenger - but hasn't gotten the message!

I observed their manly exchange high overhead as gladiator "B" marched blindly into battle and was quickly dispatched in a similar fashion, before he touched the compressor. Off he raced after gladiator A! With no one around to orient the load, I had to set it off to one side of the skid, in order to resume laughing.

Of course everyone knows *"what goes around comes around,"* and the scene for this shocking example occurred just north of Victor, Idaho on a winter seismic job. I had just finished my twenty-day stretch and was going on a ten-day break. Lourdes waited in the truck as I stopped by the magazine to say adios to "Dave," the Powder Guy. Where could he be, I wondered? He's not supposed to wander away from the dynamite.

Lo and Behold, here comes ace pilot Vern Sanders. Flying my Lama, he is hovering high over the magazine, and in need of someone to hook up a load of stump powder to his remote hook. I looked up at Vern. Vern nodded his head and grinned back down at me.

I noticed the terminus of the powder basket's wire choker lying at my feet in the wet snow, and did my pilot buddy a favor by reaching up and slapping it into the ***remo...***

I could hear Dave howling with laughter from behind a nearby tree as Vern pulled away with the basket. The static jolt I got from the Lama's rotor blades hit me like a mule kick in the gut, leaving me temporarily paralyzed - curled up like a baby in the snow. Lourdes learned a couple of new English expressions that day, and *fetal position* was among them.

HANDLES

How Captain Methane got His

In my autobiography, I tried to explain how my first employer - a fat Texas barber - used to sit on me to make me fart, solely for his entertainment. In another chapter, I wrote how my first tape recorder preserved my more legendary blasts, accompanied by two bachelor roommates. Yet, people still keep asking me, "How did you get the nickname, *Captain Methane?*" Here's how I remember it.

o   o   o   o   o

One particularly cold spring morning, I drove my trusty General Motors rig into the dark rock quarry upstream from Saint Regis, Montana - where our logging outfit parked their Hueys. Driving down the gravel incline into the Service Landing, I noted with satisfaction that everything was all lit up. That meant that "Big Al" had arisen from his trailer-camper in timely fashion; the heaters were crackling, and the generators were "ginning."

Parking near the Huey, I observed that the kerosene space heater was glowing away inside my frosty bird. I placed my helmet and lunch bucket on the padded Captain's seat, grabbed my flashlight, and reclosed the bubble door.

Stamping my snow boots as I approached the maintenance trailer, I wanted Big Al to know I had arrived. We learned the hard way to announce ourselves, so we didn't encounter each other by accident and scare each other half to death. This *was* bear country, after all.

Kicking the mud and snow off my boots outside his doorway, I heard Al mumble "Mornin' Dorce," from inside; the door was ajar. Peering in, my mechanic's brightly-lit mobile work station was just beginning to heat up. Al Martin looked up from the aircraft logbook as I entered. He smiled, offering me a white ballpoint pen to sign off the preflight inspection.

First, though, I had to perform the inspection. Back out to the ship I went, flashlight in hand. Big Al had been up long enough to remove the cumbersome main rotor blade covers and the like, a twenty-minute job for one man. I would have helped, of course. What a guy, I marveled.

I began my inspection with the left front seat area and worked my way around the nose of the old Bell/ Garlick UH-1H. Lifting open the battery access door, I surveyed the dual-battery set up. My brain slid off into *auto pilot* as my eyes scanned here and there for cracks, missing bolts, leaking cells; scores of recurring "Huey" problems were away stored in my memory banks.

It was at times like this that I would set my creative brain free to explore the wonders of the universe, without ever leaving my waffle-stompers. And for some reason that morning, my mind flew off to a cartoon I had seen days before in the newspaper. Two animal characters were arguing about whether a duck's "quack" would "echo" or not.

Why *not*, I wondered? Surely a quack would echo - given that the duck applied enough diaphragm, my Okie brain argued. It's like playing a big brass instrument – no diaphragm, no sound. I could hear old man Randall shouting at us from the Red Band director's podium, *"USE YOUR DIAPHRAGM!!"*

By that time in the inspection I had climbed atop the slippery Huey and was immersed in checking the greasy swash plate, the slimy gimbal ring, the damned damper mechanisms, etc... And conveniently another wild-haired theorem sprouted wings in my noodle.

Not only would a loud <u>quack</u> echo, so would a loud <u>fart</u>. Again, given sufficient diaphragm.

It was about then that I began reefing on that big ol' stabilizer bar that Bell bolts to their teetering rotor systems; checking some critical bearings for play. This maneuver – properly done - requires a load of body English in an attempt to bottom-out the dampers.

Somewhere in my subconscious, between summoning my considerable abdominal talent out of hiding and reefing hard on the stabilizer bar with a mighty two-fisted tug, I ceremoniously unleashed the backlog of highly pressurized byproducts from two ranch-fresh eggs over-easy with bacon, and two cups of hot sweet coffee - all at once in a powerful [QUACK?] which did *indeed* echo off the granite wall one hundred feet south of the helicopter – although it sounded oddly muffled by warm, woolen underwear.

Limping back to the maintenance trailer to sign that all-important form Big Al was saving for my signature, I realized in my zeal I had injured a sensitive area of my anatomy by *quacking* under too much pressure. As I was about to start into my noisy boot-scraping-routine outside his door, I could hear Big Al inside, and I thought I heard him crying.

When I pulled the door open to check on him, he looked up from his log book with tears in his eyes. I was surprised to see a grin on his face. He was trying not to laugh at my pagan self while christening me with my new handle, *Captain Methane* – and the quack heard 'round the quarry.'

BABBLING BOB AND THE BLACK HOLE

I first heard the nickname "Babbling Bob" from one of our louder Bell 214 mechanics. "Bruce" made it sound like Bob Stucke was a real character. This was a little like the pot calling the kettle "black," frankly. Turns out, Bob is the nicest guy; a helicopter pilot who has had a very interesting life and knows rotorcraft mechanically from the ground up. By that I mean he earned an FAA A&P Mechanic's license, a rating that started him on his way to fame and glory. Well, sort of.

Bob Stucke was not born rich, but after he became a mechanic, he was for a time married to a lady of substantial wealth and enjoyed all the privileges that go with being rich. Hardly any of his peers had much more than a brief flight in the First Class Section, but Bob had lived the life, savored the champagne, fresh King Crab and caviar while the rest of us were eating bologna sack lunches and toiling in the dust of greasy rotorcraft; or heli-logging in the Northwest over the frozen larch stands.

After his divorce came reality. Bob was back to being a working man like the rest of us. But during his life of luxury, Bob learned to fly helicopters, got his commercial rating, and some good experience to go with it. By pounding on doors and hustling, he managed to become a heli-logger in the same outfit I was working for near Aberdeen, Washington.

We flew UH-1H model Hueys in those days; single pilot, left seat. One thing you should know about heli-loggers: the four or five-man logging crews we hovered over were quick to whip a nickname on a new guy. Turns out, the "hookers" couldn't top the nickname that Bob arrived with, so they wasted no time spreading the word that the new pilot was to be known as 'Babbling Bob." Bob had a great sense of humor about all this and rolled with the radio's verbal punches all day long.

There were two logging crews working for the outfit I referred to earlier. I was on break when I got the word that Bob had crashed. The good news was, he would fully recover. A broken collarbone and facial lacerations, but mendable. Not so for his Huey, which erupted into flames –after the traumatic crash. The conflagration created a sizeable black hole in the green forest before fire crews managed to extinguish it.

"Hooker" Dirk Welsh thought he had cleared to a safe place, but when Bob applied power over Dirk's "turn" of logs, the rotorcraft's vertical pylon broke rudely off the Huey's tail boom, leaving poor Captain Stucke strapped to an uncontrollable aircraft.

The helicopter spun rapidly to the right and the naked, rotorless tail boom hit the tall trees surrounding the ship, bringing the old war bird down in a spectacular crash. Dirk was almost taken out by flying debris. Regaining his senses, Dirk radioed for help and ran to Bob's rescue, moments before a growing turbine engine-fire consumed the fuselage and surrounding trees.

Bob briefed me personally a bit later - arm in cast – after I pulled in next to his rig at the local Darrington RV Park. I had been dispatched to fly in a replacement Huey and start logging where Bob left off; clean up the logs left lying around the infamous "black hole," where Bob's Huey turned into a pile of ashes. Stucke was freshly back from the local hospital to retrieve his trailer.

Captain Bob introduced me to his pretty wife and told me all about the crash. He was in a typical broken-collarbone-cast, his left arm suspended even with the height of his left shoulder, for several weeks while he mended. He didn't have to point out the fresh pink-colored horizontal laceration across his forehead where his left door's plastic bubble window exploded, and "…almost tore (his) face off," according to Bob. Bob was a very lucky guy, and he knew it.

Bob didn't know the new nickname our logging crew had decided on, though. I caught wind of it on my CB radio as I pulled into camp. I didn't have the heart to tell him. He would find out soon enough. *Babbling Bob* would henceforth be known as *"Franken-Stucke!"*

EXORCISING THE EVIL AIRCRAFT

My 666 used to be a 206B

While flying as a 3-D Seismic helicopter pilot in the great state of Texas a few years back, I had the pleasure of navigating over some thorny range country using a patented GPS/GLONASS DynaByte processor unit. This satellite-based technology gives one the ability to navigate to within a meter of a given point with relative ease.

To those unfamiliar with this high tech system, the pilot follows directions on a small DynaByte TV screen, which interprets data from the processor unit. The latter is a toaster-oven-sized, solid-state gizmo occupying a small space in front of my 206BIII Jet Ranger's left front seat's footrest.

This complicated system is very reliable, unless there are extenuating circumstances, such as: improper programming on location, heavy cloud layers in early morning, the rare instance of satellite failure; or in my case, the *Evil Aircraft*.

I became aware of the problem around noon one day, flying west of the Brazoria Municipal Airport. I was supporting our thirty-man seismic crew by deploying their seismic jugs, batteries and cables at precise locations on the flat but densely wooded countryside. Hovering along at 130-feet, a heavy bag full of goodies was suspended from the Seis-Bag device below me, waiting to be "deployed."

Holding the payload just above some dense tree tops, I maneuvered slowly, waiting for the all-important "X" to appear on the diminutive screen, my signal that the helicopter was directly over the desired spot. Once observed, I could theoretically lower the cargo between the tree limbs, release the load and return to the staging area for another.

This was usually fast work, but for some reason, my indicator began jumping around at the moment of truth, and I couldn't come any closer to within ten feet of the magic "X." Frustrating, and somebody has to pay for unproductive flying. The ground crew, the computer, *and* the Hobbs meter would conspire to rat on my erroneous navigation. So I radioed the Staging Manager, "Houston, we have a problem!"

My Canadian staging manager was a tall, cigarette-smokin' trouble shooter, used to making hundreds of unpopular decisions a day. His reply was abrupt and to the point: *Go park that thing and get it fixed.*

Fate would have it that there was (at that time) an interesting little helicopter Fixed Base Operator near the south end of the Brazoria Airport, and bless their hearts, they had an avionics shop. It was only by sheer luck the technician was available when I appeared in his doorway during lunch, helmet in hand.

I actually had little hope that the technician knew anything about this relatively newfangled navigation gear I was having problems with, but I had to ask. "Let's take a look," the technician suggested, as we walked out to the hot transient parking apron near the taxiway.

The technician carried with him a small leather bag, much like the ones doctors of old carried when making house calls. He asked me to turn on the avionics master switch and power up the nav equipment. While I was going through the motions, he casually extracted an intriguing, palm-sized electronic device from his surgeon's kit and walked away from the Jet Ranger – out beyond the rotor's arc, where he stopped and turned around.

Pushing a button on the side of the device, the technician held it at eye level and smiled. "Ten birds," he announced, meaning there were ten navigation satellites hovering well above us, ready to go to work. He then lowered the device to navel level and walked slowly toward me, as I sat behind the right seat's controls.

The technician's pace slowed to a crawl as the device passed through the open doorway across from me. He looked very much like a *Ghost Buster*: furrowed brow, bent over his strange device, trying to interpret the data from his *exorcisor*. "Three birds," he announced, sounding disappointed. "*Evil aircraft*," he added softly. He silently switched the device off and back into the bag it went.

Knowing that true avionics wizards work best without kibitzers like me slowing them down, I piped down and watched. The crafty guy began a methodical search for the "evil," starting with the antenna that received the satellite feed. Working his way along the skin of the helicopter, he followed the wiring bundle as it looped around and entered the nose of the aircraft, via the chin-bubble's drain hole. Over the faint noise of the ship's gyros, I could hear him humming to himself as he passed inspection on centimeter after centimeter of wiring and coax-connectors.

My exorcist soon focused his attention on the area where the shielded wire-bundle made its way into the back of the processor unit. Gently pulling the wires tight, the shield pulled away from the wiring, exposing a mere ¼ inch of the bundle. "Here is your demon," he advised. "Shut it off and I'll have it fixed in an hour."

The problem, technically stated, was that the coax shield was "open" at the processor end. Signals were leaking past the opening and into the airframe. This effectively blocked seven satellites, which provided insufficient data for my equipment to work properly. With the shield reinstalled over the wiring, all ten "birds" were once again guiding my way. I was back in service - and from then on, I knew who to call!

TROJAN MOONBUS

When opportunity knocks, snap it!

Retirement brings with it a little more time to do things that please us; in my case, little or nothing - as I sit somewhat reclined in my humble patio beneath the power lines. Okay, I have a camera in my hands, and I would have a clear view of the east, were it not for the neighbor's north-south roofline. For heavenly observation, it is adequate - if you don't expect much.

Month after month, year after year, a pattern in the heavens became obvious: Just over the top of a tall pine tree at stage center, airliners approached the greater Los Angeles basin westbound - about 10,000 feet in elevation - paralleling the east-west Interstate 10, five miles south of my location.

Some of those lofty 747s and DC-10s descend from that point to a landing in Ontario, CA [ONT] Others continue on, gear up; flying at approach speed toward Los Angeles International [LAX]. I shot a few photos of them, enlarged enough to read "Quantas" or some other familiar name.

Pretty interesting stuff for an old man to toy with. I got plenty of practice trying to get a clear tripod or handheld image of anything that far away, moving at nearly 300 mph. Primetime comes as the last rays of sunlight shine eastward. In the late afternoon sun, horizontal beams over the Pacific Ocean light up westbound airliners Trojan red for a precious moment, then fade to gray.

Two months out of the year, the moon rises behind the airliners' level of flight and the drama begins. Will tonight be the night? Will a golden 747 slide straight through the moon's image, magnified by the telescopic lens - hoping beyond hope that I can trip the shutter on the fleeting image - no larger than a pea held at arm's length - and capture it?

I wasn't anticipating the sudden appearance of a low flying Airbus. Six miles away, a glowing A300 was turning southwest toward Ontario Airport, not LAX, yet it was drawing a bead on the moon. My right index finger rested on the shutter button, pressing lightly. My heart sped up a notch as the Moonbus drew me underneath the power lines.

In order to snap the red airliner, I had to shoot between the overhead wires. Bearing down on the ghostly gray orb, I was delighted to see "Captain Wonderful" bank to the left, gear up and start hauling butt. The moon went dark in my viewfinder, and my itchy finger and **Canon** did the rest.

Bingo! Not bad for an old fart.

Now Comes

Captain Methane's Hall of Honor

The chapters that follow are dedicated to specific aviators and crew members who served the US military in the Republic of South Vietnam. I knew some of these men personally. In certain instances, I have had to recreate conversations from long ago. I have done so conservatively, and to the best of my ability. In telling these brave mens' stories, I seek only to shed illumination upon their accomplishments, their valor, and their sacrifices.

Photographs of and pertinent information about
the Fallen listed below can be found on the Internet
through the following link: www.thewall-usa.com

The Fallen, in alphabetical order:

Beck, Gregory George - CW2, US Army
Casey, James - WO1, US Army
Cofer, James - SP5, US Army
Davenport, James M. - SP4, US Army
Granville, Ronald L. – SP4, US Army
Huffstutler, Steven R. – 1st Lieutenant, US Army
Pittard, David H. – Major, US Air Force

CW2 GREGORY GEORGE BECK

MOS 100E: Attack Helicopter Pilot

Camp Enari, South Vietnam/March of 1969. My orders assigned me to the 4th Infantry Division's 4th Aviation Battalion. Upon reporting for duty, the major who briefed me actually gave me my choice of flying "slicks," or "guns." Having missed out on the standard gunship training at Fort Rucker, I replied that I had no preference; but that I liked guns and I liked to shoot.

That must have been what he wanted to hear, for before very long, I was sent over to "B" Company's Gambler Guns Operations building at the east edge of the dusty flight line.

In due time, I was introduced to a genuine Attack Helicopter Pilot, CW2 Gregory George Beck. A handsome man an inch or so taller than I, "Greg" was a quarter-way through Tour Number Two of the Vietnam conflict. His first assignment had been with the First Cavalry Division. Soft-spoken and easygoing as he was, I had to listen up when he showed me around the Bell "C" model gunship I was to get checked out in.

Pilots begin with an inspection of the helicopter (the Preflight Inspection) and finish up with the rockets and guns. Greg's assigned crew chief and gunner shared most of the maintenance and armament duties. Smiling reservedly as we shook hands, the enlisted men went back to work loading linked 7.62 rounds into the main ammo tray.

"These weapons can fire six thousand rounds per minute," Greg assured me. "But if you get in a firefight, ammo goes quickly." We exchanged a respectful glance. "When you run out of bullets and rockets, you're useless as a gun platform; so we slow the guns down to about half that."

Looking on was the crew chief, who didn't seem to be all too excited about checking out a "newbie" gun pilot. The gunner avoided eye contact. Rubbing the mini-gun's cold steel barrels down absentmindedly with an oily rag, the muscular G.I. stuffed the oily rag deep into his left rear fatigue pants pocket, where it couldn't blow into the tail rotor later on.

The gunner shifted his attention to correcting the "shape" of the bullet's flex-guide coming out of the ammo tray. I felt truly awkward around somber, deeply tanned combat-hardened helicopter warriors - and all this meat-shredding machinery for the first time.

The "C" Model gunship ship always took off with maximum load. The weight of our arms almost never changed, only the fuel load and crew weight varied. Thus configured, the old gunship would barely hover out of the revetment on a hot day in the Central Highlands. Even then, it was with only two souls onboard and a lot of coaxing.

From a point of instruction, this was a classic density-altitude induced phenomenon, best illustrated by attempting to hover a max-gross Bell 204B gunship (with the heavy "540" rotor-system) backward - out of an L-shaped blast-wall revetment, without settling-with-power. It didn't help that we had to hover downwind in the process.

This maneuver was achieved without the added weight of our other two crewmembers. They wore their flight helmets and walked alongside, acting as ground guides and getting thoroughly blasted by the fine, red dust in our rotor wash. Jagged sheets of dark red dust-abatement material flipped up in the gale and *flew away like crazed Frisbees.*

Greg reminded me, "Don't stir the stick." I knew that old axiom from instrument flight training, but this was different. The ship would barely hover at max-gross in the given situation, the 'low-RPM-warning-horn' wailing in our helmets.

Mr. Beck and I were observing high exhaust-gas temperatures and gas-producer readings, but the ship felt sluggish, her cyclic response, sloppy and "unhappy." The air around us was being denied a uniform cushion due to the proximity of the revetment wall and the prevailing wind.

But the wall was there for protection against rocket and mortar attack, so we had to deal with tricky conditions to park and un-park the "C" model. On the morning we hovered out for gunnery instruction, a hot breeze was spilling over the L-shaped revetment walls; spoiling our ground cushion, big time.

A gentlemanly flight instructor, Greg, kept his hands in his lap as I did my best to smoothly hover a foot or so over the ground while coaxing the stick back ever so gently.

The low rotor RPM siren was wailing like a butt-shot banshee before I moved another inch, the ship wallowed like a foundering buffalo and settled to the ground. Putting the collective pitch lever all the way down, the engine RPM quickly recovered to 6600 and I tried again. The next effort netted us another five feet aft, and we settled again – plunk! (Damned good thing we were not on an emergency "scramble" of some kind!)

Greg kept encouraging me, and we soon had the ship pointed toward the PSP taxiway.

From this point on, the tower operator knew to be patient with the "C" Model." We needed a few seconds to get the helicopter sliding along the PSP runway, our two crewmen literally running alongside to keep their weight off the laboring rotor blades.

As the ship slid noisily along, it steadily accelerated toward the magical 18 to 20 knot translational lift airspeed. The crew scrambled onboard like gymnasts and buckled into their "monkey straps," just as the ship shuddered through translational lift. We were suddenly flying, the hot metal runway growing shorter under our low-pointing nose.

The gunnery range was southeast of Camp Enari only a kilometer or two. Greg flew from the right seat and talked me through the process as he armed the mini-guns for our first pass. Noticing some very shot-up metal junk and holey fuel drums ahead, I leaned forward and peered through the mini-guns' flex sight, zeroing in on one of the barrels. As I squeezed the trigger, the gunner behind me "went hot."

Angling his M-60 machine gun about 280 degrees outboard, he opened fire and sent a score of very hot, freshly ejected 7.62 shell casings in the direction of my jungle-fatigue shirt collar. The shells felt like French fries, fresh-out-of-the-deep-fryer; dropping down into the opening behind my neck and burning the crap out of me! The gunner knew exactly what he was doing; getting a new guy ready for combat.

In reflex, I released the sight, flailed my arms and hit the "stops" on my 4-way body harness. My immediate reaction was to reach up quickly and attempt to stand my collar straight up. Hot brass wouldn't collect there with one's collar properly positioned.

The bad thing was, I had stopped firing when the brass burned me. In combat, that could get us all killed. Nobody had to say it, and I wouldn't forget the lesson. My shirt collar stayed turned up for the duration. Both of our gunners seemed to think it was pretty funny that I got burned and acted like a flailing monkey for a second or two.

o   o   o   o   o

The Army of 1969 knew the "C" Model gun ship was lacking in performance and capability, ergo several new stripped-down Bell "Cobra" AH-1G models were arriving In Country, a boatload at a time. I learned from a correspondent that Greg had attended "Cobra Hall" between his first and second tours. Mr. Beck arrived at Camp Enari the same day as fellow Cobra grad CW2 Bruce Loughridge, and "B" Company's new CO, Major Ron Hannon.

I respected the fact that Greg never laid the "I wish we had our Cobras already" attitude on me. He took it in stride that we had to accomplish our missions with Charlie Models a bit longer; frankly, I never heard the man complain about anything.

"B" Company's Cobras did start arriving that spring, but by then, I was a "slick" pilot in training with the "A" Company Blackjacks.

All during my Gambler Guns training phase, our enemy was believed to have gone into regroup and resupply mode. There were relatively few rocket and mortar attacks around II Corps; NVA Infantry units were apparently resting up. Was Charlie waiting us out?

My brief tour as a gun pilot had been so uneventful that I had literally been lulled to sleep, flying redundant circles in the humid jungle air with a grossed-out gunship. Meanwhile, those daring slick pilots were down there working-out, flying in and out of tiny LZs with sling loads; delivering fresh troops and resupplying Fire Bases with vital ammunition and hot meals. That's what I wanted to do. Being a Gambler Gun required way too much patience.

When I first brought up the idea of flying slicks, Greg didn't seem surprised. He had to agree with me about boring holes in the sky. I had flown a few combat assaults with Mr. Beck by then. I could stay awake during one of those with no problem!

With Greg at the controls, we flew to the right of a thundering Blackjack slick formation. Our Gambler Gun sister-ship flew five hundred feet above and behind us, ready to open up with deadly hail at the drop of a hat. Friendly artillery prepped the large field ahead.

We waited anxiously for the sign that our preparatory barrage had ceased. A white artillery marker-round burst on cue, raining white magnesium remnants over the field two miles ahead, signaling the "all clear." I had the field in my sights, ready to fire our guns.

On Greg's command, I opened up with two roaring, electrically-powered mini-guns, sweeping the grassy battlefield with deafening, three-second bursts, as we accompanied the formation toward the shot-up LZ. We never did set off any booby-traps or draw counter fire. Charlie and the NVA were apparently otherwise engaged.

That said, we'd cover the formation as they landed and offloaded. Time after time, they would land swiftly and take to the air again without consequence. But as for me, "logging" five to seven flight hours took ten hours or more, strapped into the gunship's uncomfortable armored seat. Being bored out of my skull didn't help make the time pass.

So, I got it into my head to ask Greg if I could transfer to slicks. And bless him, Greg Beck paved the way for me. Before the new Cobras arrived, I was a Blackjack.

I was still a Blackjack "peter pilot," (considered still in training) a month later, the night it happened. When the rockets fell around Camp Enari for the second night in a row, most of us headed for the nearest bunker. It was approximately 7:15 in the evening, Sunday, May 18th. Dark storm clouds were headed our direction when the 122s hit northwest of our hooches.

Charlie had rocketed Camp Enari on the 17th of May, according to fellow Blackjack pilot Tim Wilkerson's nonfiction diary, <u>Clear Right! Clear Left!</u> The 18th of May barrage occurred at 5:25 PM and numbered six rockets and fifty mortars.

As fate would have it, Greg Beck was on standby with his 200-hour Cobra. His co-pilot, a relatively new man in the unit, took shelter in a bunker instead of reporting to the ship. Greg tried to find his front-seater, but accepted an eager SP5 James Cofer's offer to fly along, instead. Here is what happened next, according to various witnesses:

Bill Roberts, Lizard 7, added this report to an online military article about the incident:

"Greg was my roommate. That night (he) was on standby flying his new Cobra. I was way down at the flight line, helping with a 100-hour inspection. The rockets and mortars started coming in and they were hitting way off to the north side of Camp Enari.

The guns didn't go out for a while and finally Greg took off. We watched him silence the enemy position west of Enari and listened to the whole thing on our radio. The ceiling was real low and we could hear him come around the traffic pattern, turning west on final approach.

Greg went into the clouds. The last transmission we heard… Greg was switching his radios over to Pleiku AFB for a GCA. [Ground Controlled Approach]

We found out later, Greg had been assigned a brand new peter pilot. When the rockets started coming in, the peter pilot headed for a bunker rather than manning his ship.

Greg tried to find him and finally put the crew chief Cofer in the front seat. When he went into the clouds he was pretty busy by himself, and I believe the Cobra only had basic instruments at that time.

Greg turned north towards Pleiku, thinking he was well east of Dragon Mountain. To my recollection, the peter pilot was immediately transferred to another unit. When I got in from flying the next day, all of Greg's belongings had been removed from our "hooch."

Loach Pilot Walt Moss responded to my request for information about that evening:

"I jumped out to the west with an OH-6 when the 122s started hitting and hovered back in the storm. Cofer was my senior enlisted maintenance man. I didn't know he had gotten into the aircraft with Beck."

"I remember Beck calling his go-around and that he was breaking left. Having been in the front seat position, I understand some of what could have been going on with a non-rated individual in the front seat, with an almost nonexistent navigation package." Walt added most succinctly, "We were young then and didn't know what we didn't know."

Another OH-6 Loach took to the air on the same interdiction mission: Redleg Scout Pilot WO1 James Casey, Artillery Observer 1st Lt. Steven

R. Huffstutler, and crew chief/gunner James M. Davenport scrambled to direct artillery fire on the enemy.

The mission ended badly when the Regleg Loach crashed in the ensuing storm, killing the pilot and the lieutenant, and mortally injuring crew chief Davenport. He died a week later.

Another eye witness report came from an online post from Bill Lathan, related to the lost AH-1G, Tail Number 67-15778. Lathan was an Army Band member who went outside after the rockets stopped and saw illumination rounds in the air. He heard Beck's Cobra make what sounded like an aborted approach outside the west bunker line's perimeter wire and "saw the fireball" when the Cobra hit Dragon Mountain.

It didn't take a military genius to figure out Charlie's strategy: coordinate his attack with the arrival of a storm. The enemy launched their rockets and mortars late in the day, with light fading fast and the barometer falling. In doing so, he hoped to buy some time for his side, while minimizing the opportunity for an American counterattack. They must have celebrated in learning that the 4th ID lost five dedicated men and two valuable aircraft.

Over forty years have passed since Greg Beck gave me my golden opportunity to build my helicopter utility skills and leave the gun-slinging to someone else. It was a very unselfish thing for him to do. It also meant that Greg would have to repeat a whole month of training, and get to know another freakin' new guy all over again. But that was okay.

So with Greg's assistance, I took my chances as a slick pilot. It was very risky and I wondered more than once if I could fly with the best combat pilots in the Army and live to tell about it. Somehow, by the grace of God, I did. My hunger for the adventurous life, that of a commercial utility pilot, led me to a succession of wonderful construction projects, near and far. I have written three books about my career, celebrating a life of adventure.

Who am I supposed to thank when I look back on all the excellent times I've had since hanging up my uniform? I guess I could start with the Army recruiter who signed me up and skip to a couple of suave primary instructors, certainly. They were instructors for hire, however. CW2 Gregory George Beck flew for God, Country, and the Gambler Guns. Yet the man saw what I wanted, and set me free to pursue it.

I know that Gambler 46, Bruce Loughridge, meant well when he suggested to me that (my) "…decision to go to slicks had nothing to do with Greg flying with a non-rated person. It was an emergency scramble…" Bruce suggested very wisely that I "…not go with (that) idea." Very good advice, Bruce. The same advice I would give to any combat veteran feeling guilty about the very special people we left behind in Southeast Asia."

THE ANIMAL

Janis Joplin with a DFC

My first ninety days in Vietnam as an Army helicopter pilot included random enemy rocket attacks and several gut checks; it was easily what I signed up for, and then some. Yet despite all the regimented military training Uncle Sam threw at me, I was not prepared for the new guy they nonchalantly Jeeped over to "The Ghetto" without so much as a warning. Someone chuckled, *"Here comes your replacement, Wingo."*

The newbie pilot had a deceptively simple handle: *Stephen L. Howard*. A fair-skinned lad, he stood a few card decks shy of six feet, but built fairly stocky. Potential middle-weight boxing material in another life, but he chose to fly thin-skinned choppers for Richard Nixon instead.

Not a bad looking young Warrant Officer, once you got past the close-set, twinkly blue eyes and the energetic smirk on his face that signaled, *"I've got it all figured out, man."*

It was none other than Mike *"The Elephant Brander"* Mullenix who nicknamed young Mr. Howard "The Animal," following an exuberant binge at a rare Rock 'n Roll show in the 4th Aviation Battalion's compound late one night. After we closed the place down and were on our way back to The Ghetto, some devious Left Seater[14] in our group of four pilots pointed out a five-foot, freshly whizzed-upon rubber tree growing in the dark nearby and ordered, "***Kill!***"

Drunk as a skunk and feeling frisky, I crouched low, made like a Roman wrestler, and beat feet for the helpless tree. But before I could karate chop the immature vegetable, Steve Howard flew past me like the *Tasmanian-Devil-on-self-destruct*. Our spirited newbie block-tackled the poor plant and quickly chewed it asunder at its pissy stump, while the rest of us stood there with our jaws hanging wiiiide open.

---

[14] The Huey's left seat was normally the command pilot's first choice, *ergo* he's a Left Seater.

Mullenix was the first to break the lull in verbal intercourse: "**Steve Howard**, *you're a **f-ing** <u>animal!!</u>*" he ordained, as the rest of us hooted. Mr. Howard had earned his nickname in grand style. We helped levitate said terrible termite from a small pile of rubber plant debris, and continued on our merry way.

"The Animal" quickly learned that regardless of skull-pounding hangovers, helicopter warriors get up early, grab their guns, chow down & coffee up and make a *beeline* for the *flight line*. A closed-door briefing in the white S-2 building, then it's off to our war-birds, where it'll be many long hours in the saddle before most of us perform our post-flights, debrief, and walk bow-legged back to "A" Company's barracks. Bow-legged and thirsty!

Built in an old ARVN camp, "A" Company occupied ten crude wooden hooches under two long sheet-metal roofs. With two field urinals between the structures, it had an air all of its own. The place was of such dubious distinction that someone had righteously named it "The Ghetto" long before I arrived.

The Animal, Frank Gimbel and Dave Ruhlman occupied the hooch on the southwest corner of the compound. Theirs was a rat-infested hovel, known for its black lights, psychedelic posters, loud music, and a 24/7 party attitude.

Yes, it is true. Sooner or later, the average helicopter birdman was granted a day off to unlace his stinking boots, get comfortable, tilt a few beers, and catch some rays. "*Uniform of the day: shower shoes and a light coat of oil.*"

Since there was usually little spending money and no place to go, a friend or two of mine would start out by taking the short inclined walk up to the 4th Aviation Battalion Officers Club, such as it was. We'd grab a stool at the bar or sit around the little card tables, stacking up our empty beer cans while describing gorgeous women we allegedly slept with and swapping manly helicopter war stories. Later on, we would zigzag back on down to the fragrant Ghetto.

Serious leisure time included stripping down to the bare minimums and spreading out on the makeshift rocket-boxes built over and around the sandbag blast-wall. *Bare minimums* to a guy like The Animal meant a partially rolled-up, (olive drab) Army boot sock, snuggled up to his pubic hair and nothing else but the aforementioned light coat of oil.

In truth, the beer and tanning oil had only begun to flow in The Ghetto that sunny day. Meditating in silent repose, The Animal was just getting warmed up for his big opus.

o   o   o   o   o

Born in Chillicothe, Missouri on the 4th of July, 1947, Steve Howard came from a happy family who rarely turned on the radio on family trips. Steve tells me his father Jearold and mother Maxine always *sang* their way around the country-side.

In time, Steve and his sister Becky sang lead for a seven-piece band known as *The Dave Bolle Soul Review*. The talent-heavy group was popular, winning the 1968 Columbia, Missouri *Best of the Bands* competition. Steve and Becky belted out the hard-hitting tunes of blues artists James Brown, Janis Joplin, and Big Brother and the Holding Company - among others.

The senior Howard was an aircraft mechanic for James Smith McDonnell. The aircraft manufacturer of legend was secretly developing the first prototype F-4 Phantom jet fighter for the military. The firm became known as McDonnell Douglas in 1967.

Steve's father passed his enthusiasm for flying machines along to his son, as well. Steve's dad took him to see the prototype Phantom at the tender young age of fifteen. It was an eye-opening experience for young Stephen, setting him up for an encounter with fate.

Athletics also played a role in Steve's character-building. He played back-up quarterback and linebacker on his high school football team, the Wentzville *Indians*. On his first fill-in for the injured starting quarterback, Steve was nervous, but calmly called the first play. It was a *Student-Body-Right, right-end-reverse*. The right end took Steve's handoff and found a seam, scoring a touchdown. It was on the field of play that young Mr. Howard learned the meaning of confidence, teamwork, determination, and personal sacrifice.

An intelligent youth, Stephen was briefly interested in studying medicine. He admittedly "partied" his way through two years at St. Mary's College in O'Fallon, Missouri. Transferring to the four-year University of Missouri, Steve's medical ambitions collided with a tough course known as *Comparative Anatomy*. *The Animal* was having a great time in college, but he was flunking Premed.

The military Draft for Vietnam was heating up. Steve's academic shortfall in the spring of 1968 came to a head when the Draft Board reclassified him "1A." As if by decree, when college "finals" rolled around, Stephen Lee Howard received his Draft Notice.

With draft notice in hand, Steve went to the local city shopping mall where the various military services had recruitment offices open for business. Set on getting into the pilot's seat, he began inquiring about their respective flight school minimums. The Air Force, Navy, and Marines mandated a college degree, period. *End of story.* Seeing no Coast Guard recruiter around, only the Army was left. - Fate turns in Mr. Howard's direction!

Steve's departure from the Marine recruiter's office was expedited by an untimely remark uttered by a frustrated would-be aviator who couldn't seem to get his toe in the door. Steve found a totally different reception at the Army recruiter's station. There, he received a warm welcome, acknowledgement of his draft notice, and a *"thanks for coming in."*

When Steve divulged his level of formal education [a two-year Associated Arts degree] and his choice for a military *dream sheet*, the recruiter seemed impressed. After a brief pause, the recruiter asked Steve, *"Have you considered flying helicopters? The Army needs chopper pilots!"* Something clicked in Steve Howard's head. Did fate put the words into his mouth? *"When can I sign up?"* Steve inquired.

After a daylong Army flight physical at nearby Fort Leonard Wood to make sure an old back injury wouldn't derail *Plan A*, Mr. Howard and fate were suddenly on a converging course over Southeast Asia. As the enemy's *Tet Offensive* reared its ugly head in South Vietnam, Steve Howard raised his right hand and became a soldier in the U. S. Army.

o o o o o

The Animal could be alarming, charming and disarming, and I can assure you that the young man loved to fly. We once hopped over to Pleiku Air Force Base in an idle "D" model Huey, our first flight together. There was always a load of soldiers catching rides both ways, supplies to haul and the like. It was like a rare *day off* with a Huey to fly around.

I remember Steve's enthusiasm matched his flying skills, at least for the basic stuff we did together. Pilots were always comparing who could land the smoothest, hover motionless like a hummingbird, take off with a heavily loaded "slick" while pulling the least amount of power, or displaying some expertise in handling random emergencies.

Steve was good, but he was in the same steep learning curve we all went through. Our personal mission was to learn fast and earn enough experience to upgrade to *Left Seat*, or *Pilot in Command* status. Today was a joyride, but in the future, Mr. Howard would be tested at every turn. On a special day in 1970, he would match wits with an infuriated NVA infantry battalion.

Back to the sun-tan-in-progress: someone has moved a loud Japanese-stereo-tape-deck and amplifier (wired to twin speakers) outside. When cranked up to around "9" on the volume dial, it was sufficient to rock the Ghetto from one end to the other - with just the right amount of distortion to sedate the average helicopter pilot. Wherever the brass was that day, I have no idea. We partied better without 'em.

In full view of the domestic hooch maids (who were hand-washing our moldy green GI shorts in the sultry shade), The Animal displayed himself face up in the dazzling sunlight of the Central Highlands. His white and hairy self was exposed, and beginning to tan.

The music of the day was The Animal's favorite: Janis Joplin, backed by Big Brother and the Holding Company. Epic booze and blues from the Sixties, man. A folded green towel shielded the Animal's eyes from the blazing sun as he turned slightly, baring a new expanse of white meat, while he leisurely readjusted his dork-sock with his left hand. Feeling around with his right, the Animal tracked down another cold Pabst; the contents of The Animal's ice-filled cooler seemed to be always within his reach.

Once the appropriate level of sunstroke and inebriation had been reached, Janis' torch song - *Ball and Chain* - started winding through the tape player. Little did we know the new guy had the whole thing in his noodle, including when Joplin smashed (her) whiskey glass off-stage, late into the song. Although he preferred Jimi Hendrix's songs, The Animal had Joplin's *fingernails-on-chalkboard* vocals down pat. And I have to admit, he could really pull it off.

Say, whoa, whoa, whoa, whoa - honey this can't be!
……..

No, no, no, no, no, no, no…..yeah, yeah, hey!

……..

*It's gonna feel just like a ball, ball, ball, oh daddy,
…and a chain!*

And the hooch maids? Man, would the Vietnamese cusswords fly! The shrieking girls squished the dirty red water out of our laundry and tried unsuccessfully to ignore him. But when *The Animal* rose dramatically to his bare feet, clutching his air-microphone with both hands atop the gritty blast wall, the sock bobbing in rhythm as he sang, matching Janis in the climactic chorus: ***whoa whoa whoa whoa whoa!***

At that point in time, the hooch maids went mostly bananas, as did anyone else gathered 'round. We were laughing hard now, knowing full well we might die at any time…violently. Acts like the Animal's are hard to find out in the field, so you might appreciate why, following his *Green Sock Debut*, we held our blues-singing newbie in such high regard.

Shift forward to my impending departure, a few months later: Camp Enari is no longer the 4th Infantry Division's headquarters. Every tank, helicopter, potato peeler, and garbage can has moved east over the Mang Yang Pass to An Khe, also known as the *Golf Course*.

When the Battalion's fleet of forty-eight helicopters started their engines in unison that cool February morning, the large, swirling rotors mixed hot exhaust gases with the surrounding cool air, and in seconds, the formation was enveloped in a dense layer of fog. I voiced my concern that this would be a bad time for the enemy to strike.

Soon the fog scattered, however, and the thundering herd headed east out of Camp Enari, following old Route 19. Those flying in the massive formation eventually got a good look at the Pass's notorious display of weathered white grave markers, the remnants of the once proud French *Groupement Mobile No.100*.[15]

Following the massacre in June of 1954, the Viet Minh buried hundreds of the dead French soldiers in an upright position. So entombed, they would face toward their homeland faraway for all time. It was a sobering reminder of our enemy's grim determination.

---

[15] Mobile Group 100 was ambushed near Km. 15 by the 803rd Viet Minh Regiment, resulting in terrible losses on the French side, including all their artillery and half of their weapons.

In moving east to An Khe, the 4th Divisions' orders were opposite of those given to the commander of the Mobile Group 100, who was ordered to leave An Khe and move to Pleiku in order to avoid hostilities. The 4th Division was to operate close to the coast for the long-range plan: shipping everything and everybody home. This is what President Nixon called "the Vietnamization of the campaign."

In one final poker game the night before I left, I cleaned house with a *full house*. I remember Captain Slack sitting there with his mouth agape; his *flush* had finished a close second. My winnings almost made up for my losses many months before.

Hauling my heavy duffel bag toward the noisy C-123J that was loading up at the flight line the next morning, I waved *adios* and wished the best of luck to my comrades-in-arms, The Animal especially.

Steve had made Left Seat before I shipped out and was a favorite with the other pilots and enlisted soldiers as well. He sported a colorful replica of *The Tasmanian Devil* with the words *"The Animal"* hand-painted on the back of his olive drab flight helmet. It was custom made by yours truly, a favor to my favorite new guy.

Thirty-five years or so later I'm in the head, reading the latest quarterly issue of The VHPA *Aviator*[16], and I can't believe my eyes: a former 4th ID Army Ranger who had served in our neck of Vietnam in 1970 had written in, trying to locate (and I paraphrase) *the brave Blackjack pilot who pulled (him) and several other guys out of a certain death situation*. He distinctly remembered the pilot had *The Animal* painted on the back of his olive drab flight helmet.

I heard about the frantic mission that earned Steve the coveted DFC[17] from the man himself, not long after we were unexpectedly reunited in the spring of 1974. I had just unpacked in yet another pink motel room in Madera, California, having been on the road for, and employed by, Evergreen Helicopters for a few months.

Del Smith had us flying six of his pretty Bell 205A-1's on a central California frost-protection contract. I was hanging around that evening on the second-story balcony when Evergreen's Ford crew-cab pickup pulled

---

[16] Vietnam Helicopter Pilot Association's quarterly magazine.
[17] Distinguished Flying Cross

into the motel parking lot, fresh from the Sacramento airport. The driver had gone to pick up a new pilot.

I could scarcely believe who walked from the crew-cab and into the light: *the Tasmanian Devil* himself, Steve Howard! A civilian now, he was standing there looking right at me, grinning - along with those beady eyes of his. Ha!

I couldn't help but yell out *"Animal!"* and laughed out loud at having an old friend back in the flock. Steve was soon debriefing me over dinner and the first thing I wanted to know was how he and our old "A" Company's *Blackjacks* fared once I left.

Steve commented on a few of the guys we both knew and that they all had made it home safely, which was great news. Steve had extended his stay In Country an additional six months with the 937th Engineers Group, taking advantage of the Army's "Early Out" program being offered to pilots who stayed on for an additional six months.

But the real story I wanted to hear was the action that earned my friend the Distinguished Flying Cross. Once The Animal began his recounting of the perilous mission in mention, he had my rapt attention.

Operating out of 4th ID's new An Khe base, Howard's mission for the first half of the day was spent inserting and extracting LLRP teams. We have no record of who was flying right seat for *Blackjack 21* that day, nor the Specialist 5th Class crew chief on board. His door gunner was a favorite, Specialist 4th Class "Billy" Battles.

Specialist Battles had crewed for me on more than one mission. He was famous for hot-rodding his M-60 machine gun by filing down the ejector chute and double-springing the action to jack up the rounds-per-minute ratio. When Battle went "hot," he really put the lead out.

Once the morning's LLRP movements were accomplished, Mr. Howard was dispatched to Landing Zone (LZ) "Hard Times," a $7/15^{th}$ Artillery fire base, twenty kilometers northeast of An Khe. They were waiting for two of their *Gambler Guns* ships to return from a medevac mission.

Howard and his crew had been standing-by less than an hour when a Staff Sergeant with a PRC-25 field radio came running up to the helipad. The E6 had just received word that one of his $K/75^{th}$ Infantry Army

Ranger SRRP[18] teams had shot an enemy soldier, the point man for an NVA Battalion. Vastly outnumbered, the Rangers were literally running for their lives and firing over their shoulders as they fled through the jungle, pleading for an emergency extraction.

Quick as a whip, Mr. Howard, the sergeant, and Steve's *Blackjack 21* crew launched out of LZ Hard Times, eastbound. There was no hesitation, no drawing of straws. As Steve put it to me so succinctly, "It would have been signing their death warrants, had we not gone after them."

Once at altitude, Howard selected "Guard" on his UHF radio, requesting any helicopter gun ship in the vicinity to "come up" on his tactical frequency. As luck would have it, there were three Bell "Charlie" Model gunships transiting the area in two different flights *and* they were armed and dangerous. Quickly, all four helicopters joined up on *Blackjack 21's* tactical frequency and headed toward the imperiled Rangers.

With the belief that he was rescuing a six-man SRRP team, Steve flew over the vicinity of the fleeing Rangers, making radio contact. The Rangers were holed up among some large boulders at the east end of a nasty box canyon. Enemy soldiers were firing at the Rangers while others ran west along the southern exposure to head off any rescue attempt.

The slopes surrounding the box canyon stood around 3,000 feet high and were "ugly, with gnarly trees and rocks," according to Steve. The Animal requested *Ranger Lead* to "pop smoke" while he circled out of the range of small arms fire. Identifying the color of smoke, Mr. Howard instructed the Rangers to hunker down. *"I'm comin' to get you!"*

The three gunships were quick to set up a racetrack pattern an appropriate distance north of the smoke, enabling them to rain down scores of 2.75" high explosive aerial rockets and buckets of hot lead from six mini-guns onto the tree-lined ridge above the trapped Rangers. Steve made a rapid descent at the west end of the canyon, using the terrain for cover the best he could.

Demanding maximum military power, Steve built up airspeed as the Huey low-leveled over the canyon's narrow meadow, then cyclic-climbed rapidly toward the rocky LZ. Machine gun fire from the right tree line sent green tracer-rounds streaking through the open cargo doors, over the prone Sergeant lying on the floor with his M-16 in hand.

---

18   SRRP – Short Range Reconnaissance Patrol – known as "Slurps."

Billy Battles opened up on the right-side M-60 machine gun as he saw tracers arcing down in their direction. Steve was comforted for an instant, hearing the SP4's hot-rod machine gun spit lead. Just as quickly, Battles' infamous gun ceased firing, and The Animal feared the worst.

"*Billy! Billy, are you okay?!*" Steve shouted over the bedlam. Battles responded with an apology, all-the-while snatching the M-16 from the Staff Sergeant's hands and firing back at the bad guys. "*I'm sorry, Mr. Animal – the bolt flew out!*" Battle's M-60 ejector chute failed, shooting the gun's bolt off into the jungle below.

As Battles returned fire with the M-16, Steve Howard pulled hard aft on the cyclic in order to hop over a row of trees that obscured the rocks on the uphill side. When the Huey came to a brief, tail-low hover, tracers flew by the nose of the ship from right to left. Simultaneously, the lead "Charlie" Model gunship opened up with several aerial rockets. The roaring rockets zipped over the hovering Huey as Steve maneuvered for a one-skid landing on a boulder.

With six aboard and ready to lift out, to his great surprise, Howard saw six more exhausted K/75 Rangers hunkered behind a pile of large boulders. Steve reefed in the horsepower for take-off, knowing he and his crew would have to risk everything one more time to save the others.

As if by a miracle, another *Blackjack* slick pilot, CW2 Homer Atwell had been monitoring the frequency and, although shot-up in an earlier skirmish, Atwell was suddenly on scene in a repaired bird - and he had observed *Blackjack 21's* immaculate extraction from a distance.

"*What'cha doin' Animal?*" Howard heard a familiar voice and distinct southern drawl over the *Blackjack* frequency. "*Need some help?*"

Steve replied to the affirmative while diving downslope to the east, in clear view of the Phu Cat Air Force Base. Heeding Steve's admonition to approach the LZ downwind and use a prominent boulder for a skid-landing, Atwell and crew bravely headed into the heat of battle. Under the cover of those unforgiving gunships, Homer made the final extraction of six weary Rangers without taking any hits.

There was great, soul-rending celebration aboard the two laboring *slicks* as their human cargo headed safely away from the dogs of war and the jaws of fate. Dave Bristol, one of the happy Rangers on board, noted my colorful rendering of "Taz" on the helmet of the valiant pilot flying left seat, a sight he would never forget.

So now you know a bit about a couple more American heroes, and I can assure you that Steve Howard and Homer Atwell were honored the next morning at what is known in combat parlance as an *"Impact Award."* When American valor is obvious and the enemy is soundly repulsed, the military responds with appropriate recognition.

Steve and Homer received the Distinguished Flying Cross from Major General Pepke, the 4th Infantry Divisions' Commanding General, in a private meeting. It must have been a proud moment for them - as well as my old unit- to save the Rangers' bacon, with no losses on our side. The two *Blackjack* co-pilots, by the way, would also receive DFCs, after due process.

With the Battalion's two companies standing in neat rows at parade rest in the assembly area, Warrant Officers Stephen Lee Howard and Homer Atwell were presented with the Army's seventh highest military decoration. *General Orders Number 2393* was read aloud by an officer from a fresh set of orders: [Quoting from the latter half of the Order]...

"For heroism while participating in aerial flight, then Warrant Officer Howard's craft began receiving fire. Undaunted, W.O. Howard landed and completed the extraction without his helicopter being hit or anyone on board injured. W.O. Howard's exceptional courage, professional skill and exemplary devotion to duty are in keeping with the finest traditions of the military service and reflect great credit upon himself, his unit, and the United States Army."

Steve reported a strange occurrence inside the An Khe "Golf Course" perimeter wire the following evening. Apparently reeling from stinging losses during the Rangers' rescue:

"...enemy sappers penetrated the base's perimeter near the 1st of the 10th Cavalry's flight line. The Officer of the Guard [OG] on duty that night foolishly assigned a Conscientious Objector (C.O.) to man a guard tower on the perimeter. The C.O. saw the sappers. Being a REAL C.O., he interfered with a fellow soldier in the tower who raised his M-16 to stop the sappers. During the brief scuffle, the sappers made it through.

The sappers spread themselves out along the flight line. As a general alarm sounded, they ran to every flyable helicopter's revetment. Interestingly, they skipped the ships that were in need of maintenance.

When the sappers reached a revetment, they would open one of the cockpit doors and toss in a satchel charge. Closing the door again for maximum effect, they would take off for the next revetment. The satchel-charges were timer-detonated, giving the sappers several seconds to clear. Steve said he and others in the bunker that morning could hear the very unusual sound of fueled-up Loaches and Hueys exploding on the ramp.

The sappers rapidly depleted their inventory of explosives. Grabbing some rocks, they made it to where the hated Cobras were parked. Opening up the canopies and climbing inside, they took out their frustrations on all the instruments they could smash. Charlie was trying to get even for something."

Mr. Howard's Huey - update: Days after the incident, Steve's crew chief was still in disbelief. So many bullets whizzed by that day, yet they took not even *one* round? Following a hunch, he searched the ship once more and located a fresh bullet hole. An enemy's rifle round had impacted a hardened doubler in the transmission wall, inches from where Billy Battles manned his M-60 machine gun.

After completing his regular 12-month tour and volunteering for another six months with the 931'st Engineer Group, Steve finally returned home as a civilian.

Steve admittedly had a tough time adjusting to life off the battlefield and told me of some of the soul-searching he underwent, trying to make a living as a Certified Flight Instructor flying an old Bell 47.

The civilian versions tell of how Howard and Wingo flew one of Evergreen's Hueys cross-country one night to a forest fire in the northwestern USA, months after our reunion in Madera. I remember being totally exhausted as the long flight over tall, unseen mountain peaks ground on and on, but Steve seemed to have hit the wall hours back, and kept right on going. *"What an animal,"* I thought to myself, as I scanned the inky blackness around us.

Like the warrior that he is, Steve kept his nose to the stone. So much for fires, though. After three years in Africa fighting the *River of Blindness Fly* for the World Health Organization, Evergreen put the young pilot to work flying Twin Otters in Alaska.

From there, Steve transitioned to Flight Engineer on Evergreen 727s and eventually made the big jump to the airliner cockpit in 1982. Steve's career as an airline pilot was finally off the ground and climbing steadily. By then, Steve and his first wife, Betty, had two children by the names Nicole and Chris.

Steve began flying for United Airlines in 1985. He retired twenty years later with a proud record and over 24,000 flight hours, flying *the friendly skies*.

In addition to his FAA Commercial Rotorcraft and ATP, Captain Howard holds the following ratings: SK-61 Type; Multi Engine Land; Boeing 727, 737, 747-400; 757, and 767 endorsements.

I was honored to attend Captain Howard's surprise retirement party in Denver in 2005, and *what a crowd* showed up to honor this guy. I was not surprised that he and his second wife Kathy had such a large flock of enthusiastic friends.

When it was my turn to roast my old Vietnam "newbie," I wasted little time describing aloud to everyone how we crossed paths in Vietnam and how The Animal would strip down to his basic "uniform" in order to get a good tan. At which time I carefully hoisted a dusty, wrinkled, green sock out of my bag of tricks with a long pair of kitchen tongs!

CAPTAIN MICHAEL P. "MIC" O'CONNOR

Don't never, ever shoot at a Cobra

When my Veteran helicopter friends began to flock together via that popular Internet social media tool, it was inevitable that Mic O'connor's name would pop up. I thought to myself, 'I know that guy!' So I "friended" him.

However, my normally excellent long term memory's synchro seemed to jamb every time I tried to "place" Mic. Though his name was familiar, I was unable to make a connection with a place or an event. We are both Scot-Irish by heritage, I deduced. I knew of no relatives by that name, however. I doubt we ever flew together. Surely I'd remember that.

Turns out we had both worked for Evergreen Helicopters in the mid-1970s. But in the early stages of our mutual employment, Mic went one way [large helicopters, i.e. Sikorsky Sky cranes] - while I was content with flying Hueys. Either way, there were finally some flying jobs for us Vietnam vets.

Once I discovered that my Facebook friend had earned a Silver Star and a DFC during his first tour of duty, I dearly wanted to document his heroism in this book. We finally got together in July, 2012.

Mic flew down space-available to see me from his home in the Northwestern U.S. Silver haired, mustached and handsome as ever, I was happy to finally see Michael P. O'connor sitting across the table from me in Lulu's kitchen.

I was satisfied that we had, in fact, met before; somewhere in Oregon, maybe? But any memories of our connection almost forty years before failed to light up the dark "O'connor" file, lost somewhere in my cranium - mired in a thick cloak of plaque. It dawned on me that I would have to ask Mic where our friendship began; a confession I found embarrassing, frankly.

To get us started, Mic fielded several biographical questions from my prepared outline. Having shared the experiences of Army flight school, combat in Vietnam, and Evergreen Helicopters, we rapidly filled blank after blank, scribbled onto several white pages. I had to stop my energetic former Airline Captain now and then to recant, as I got lost in the details of two poignant aerial battles.

I don't use a tape recorder for interviews, so the process of debriefing a stellar individual such as Mic O'connor took a while. But all the way through, he was friendly and relaxed as he addressed dangerous situations that could have ended differently in the blink of an eye. Many good men were lost that way.

Pausing later in the afternoon, our guest enjoyed a cold Pacifico while feasting upon a steaming plate of my wife's wonderful chicken mole, freshly prepared from her mother's old Sinaloa recipe. The questions got easier after that, and here is what I learned:

Michael P. O'connor was born December the 8th, 1947, in Seattle Washington.

"Mic," as he was called, was the baby in a family of three kids, one each brother and sister. Their father, Edward, served as an Army Air Corps major in WWII. He flew the classic P-51 Mustang. After the war, Mr. O'connor worked for General Electric and became part-owner in a speedy Aeronca airplane. He kept his wings dusted off flying around the northwest, often taking his three kids along with him.

Mic's flying lessons started early in life. With his dad in the left seat, Mic would sit on his sister Joanne's lap in the right seat and work the flight controls. Such arrangements were not without peril, as Joanne was known to barf!

It turns out that young Mic O'connor was an athlete, earning a football scholarship, right out of Sheldon High School. It was off to Oregon State afterward, where he majored in Liberal Arts and Marketing Management. Mic played quarterback on OSU's "Frosh" Team, and defensive back ["safety"] on the celebrated 1967 team – the one that the media dubbed "The Giant Killers."

Andros, the talented Beavers beat the heavily favored USC Trojans - with infamous Heisman Trophy winner O.J. Simpson in the backfield - 3 to 0 in Corvallis. The celebration was huge, but Mic had little time to party.

Within days of the victory - and needing twelve elusive credits to graduate - Mic was compelled to sign up with the US Army, in lieu of an impending draft notice.

During his medical exam to qualify for flight school, Mic became aware of his superior eyesight, evaluated as "20:10." What an advantage this would prove to be. With Mic's winning record, keen eyesight and quarterbacking skills, such talent would inevitably tip the scales of fate over the battlefield.

Private O'connor completed his Basic Training at Louisiana's infamous Fort Polk. On the heels of that came his appointment to Fort Wolter's coveted Warrant Officer Rotary Wing Aviator's Course, landing in rotation with Class 68-519/68-35. Mic graduated near the top of his "Gray Hats," earning a green light into the Army's new Cobra attack helicopter. It was then November of 1968.

Once Mic completed the six week Cobra School, his Military Occupational Specialty [MOS] changed to "100E – Attack Helicopter Pilot." Next came war.

After a long plane ride over the Pacific Ocean and the usual confusion of in-processing, Mic found a home with the 116th Assault Helicopter Company in Cu Chi, "IV Corps," South Vietnam. Mic flew "slick" Hueys for three weeks with the Hornets. He was shot down an amazing four times in his first four weeks, earning the handle, "Magnet Ass."

His company also lost three gunships during this period, creating a shortage of gun pilots. In only his fourth week In Country, Mic was suddenly piloting a Bell UH-1C gunship, flying in support of the 25th Infantry Division. His radio call sign was "Stinger 91." He also answered to "Meat."

In July of that year while piloting a UH-1C gunship, Mic alertly spotted an enemy 12.7MM anti-aircraft position hidden under camouflage among the long green rows of a large pineapple plantation. The enemy was moments away from ruining the whole day for the 101st Airborne's CMAC

Saigon Defense Team, or anyone escorting slicks into any nearby landing zones.

Only minutes before, Mic had been informed that the departure of his troop-loaded slicks had been delayed at the rear. Mic confirmed the setback and peeled away from the proposed LZ, taking his team of three UH-1C gunships out for a quick recon of the surrounding terrain. He would take another look around for the enemy before returning to drop smoke for the lumbering Hueys.

Mic's sharp eyes had actually uncovered the latest addition to a two-company-sized unit of enemy soldiers, secretly digging tunnels and setting up anti-aircraft guns for an approaching NVA battalion. By spotting the 12.7 heavy gun, Mic discovered the threat before the trap was sprung on our troops.

Without giving away his plan of attack, Mic circled in the distance, using his radio to locate a FAC (Forward Air Controller) who quickly directed Air Force fighter-bombers into the fray. Before the day was over, two flights of nine combat loaded Hueys were added to the fight. It was a bad day for the enemy.

For Mic's heroics that fateful day, he was awarded the Silver Star.

On November 1st, 1969, AH-1G Cobra pilot 1st LT Kerry B. Shive (also known as the "front-seater") and W01 Mic O'connor (aft-seater/Aircraft Commander) were flying in a Team action with fellow Cobra pilot Mike Ward, approximately ten miles east of Cu Chi.

Trang Bang for the 25th Infantry Division's "Wolfhounds," Mic was alerted that his ground unit had come into contact with an enemy unit of unknown size and had them pinned down, just east of the (north-south) road they were patrolling.

Asking for the Fire Team's support, Mic sized up the situation and began his attack. The enemy gunners were believed to be hiding along the tree-lined road and firing southeast into the friendly position.

O'connor maneuvered his Cobra into a north-bound strafing run. Firing from the Cobra's nose turret, 40MM grenades ripped into the dense canopy, along with the Cobra's merciless mini-guns. Two passes appeared to silence the shooters.

Following Mic's unopposed flight over the ambushers' position, the U.S. Commander on the ground sought the Fire Team's help in performing a BDA, or bomb damage assessment. Mic radioed that he would do so, though such work is usually left to "Loaches," the smaller two-man Scout ships. [None around!]

Swooping low and hovering along over the roadway, Mic and Kerry were finding dead enemy combatants scattered among their makeshift reinforcements in the shattered trees below. Those guys would fight no more.

Suddenly Mic's sharp eyes detected several camouflaged enemy soldiers rise up out of the brush to his Cobra's left. One enemy soldier in particular got Mic's attention; he was aiming a CHICOM Soviet RPD Type 56 machine gun at him, with its distinctive 100 round drum of ammunition!

Mic and his front-seater instantly realized their sitting-duck situation, just as over fifty man-killing bullets began impacting the canopy and left side of the stricken Cobra.

The bubble-canopy shattered with each bullet's impact as more hot lead tore through Mic's instrument panel, narrowly missing Kerry Shive. Shive shoved the Cobra's stubby cyclic stick forward and pulled power, peeling off rapidly to the northeast as the enemys' guns followed their wounded bird.

Sizing up things in the back seat, Mic realizes he has been hit by shrapnel on his left hand as other rounds ricocheted inside his angled armored seat, wounding him in the right shoulder. He could hear all the chaos from his radios, but couldn't transmit to either his front-seater or the overhead Cobra.

As Lt. Shive radioed his predicament to the overhead Cobra, Mike Ward came quickly alongside Mic's damaged machine, surveying the bullet strikes from close range. Mike Ward radioed to the Lieutenant that he could see blood trailing from the Mic's shot-up cockpit, which could only be bad news.

This is the about the same time Mic O'connor correctly evaluated that: (A) His wounds were not mortal (B) It was still his aircraft and (C) If his Cobra had any munitions left that would still fire, he was by-god-going to deliver it to the bad guys!

"My Aircraft!" Mic shouted at Lt. Shive over the bedlam. The Lieutenant must have been shocked to feel the controls wiggle and hear Mic's exclamation.

Regaining control from the aft seat and peeling away from the formation, Mic doubled back to the enemy's location, selecting "salvo" of his remaining aerial rockets the appropriate response.

When the eerie sounding, swerving Stinger 91 suddenly reappeared high over the tree, diving at the disbelieving North Vietnamese, every rocket that they had missed came streaking down upon on them, dramatically ending the battle.

With three damaged 2.75-inch rockets still hanging from the left wing's rocket pod, Mic was directed to the 12th Evac heli-pad at Cu Chi, then re-directed to the Bunker Line. Sitting in his armored seat, Mic was attended to by a flight surgeon on the scene.

While being bandaged, an Army Explosive Ordnance Disposal sergeant came running over to the Cobra carrying a big-ass hammer, whereupon he began pounding on the business end of Mic's damaged seventeen-pound high-explosive warheads like a certified maniac.

The sergeant [fresh out of Catch-22?] was taught that aerial rockets had to fly a certain distance from the pod in order to arm themselves. Mic and the surgeon could hardly appreciate their combat comedian, nor his stupid hammer.

<u>After-action footnotes:</u>

- Mic's Cobra had to be trucked to maintenance. It was too shot up (and bloody) to fly.
- Mic got two days of rest, then it was back in the saddle with him.
- A timely assessment of the enemy's last stand produced Mic's newest war trophy, the very same RPD machine gun that had wounded him. It was retrieved by the ground unit, somewhat scorched and twisted out of shape by Mic's accurate salvo of "rockets."
- Pilot O'connor was awarded the Purple Heart for his unwavering sense of duty and decisiveness in this particular battle. The Army brass also recognized Mic's leadership abilities, offering the young Warrant Officer a direct commission to 1st Lieutenant in the Army's Armor Corps, hardly a month later.

Mic left Vietnam in Jan. of 1970. He was assigned to Fort Wolters and became a Primary Instructor Check Pilot. In May of 1970, Mic received his Armor training.

Lt. O'connor returned to Vietnam to serve with the 334th AHC as a Cobra pilot, call sign "Dragon 32," through the end of 1971. By the time Mic packed up for the states, he had been awarded the following decorations for his service in the war zone:

Silver Star; The Distinguished Flying Cross; The Purple Heart; Bronze Star; Vietnamese Air Cross for Gallantry, with Palm; and a fistful of Air Medals.

After his second tour in the war zone, Mic was stationed in Germany, serving with the 334th ASC for his last two years in uniform. He became a civilian in 1974. After touring Europe's historic destinations with a lady friend, he finished his Marketing Management degree at Texas Christian University and became a commercial helicopter pilot.

I learned something else that Mic O'connor and I both had in common: an encounter with movie director John Landis. One must remember that I was at the controls of a helicopter that crashed disastrously on Landis' movie set in 1982.

Mic had left the world of commercial helicopters by the time my lengthy Twilight Zone movie trial was over. He and I had both lost good friends due to a plague of helicopter accidents in the 1980s. Mic decided to take his Airline Transport and Boeing 737 Rating and leave the rotating wing fraternity.

The new Mic would revert back to flying airplanes, like his dad. He had to start at the bottom and work up. His employer had a lot of airplanes: F-28s, BE-99s, Dash-8 Dehavillands, Bombardier 700s. Years later, he was an official Airline Captain.

Which brings us to a flight Mic was commanding, destined for Reno, Nevada. He was taking on passengers one afternoon at busy Los Angeles International Airport. This was in the day before the infamous 9-11 terrorist attacks, so anyone walking in the left-forward passenger entrance could see into the cockpit via their wide-open door.

According to Mic, an inebriated John Landis barged uninvited into the cockpit, where he took on a Marx Brothers' character. Sizing-up the cockpit, Landis announced that he "…was making sure that he was flying with a competent pilot."

Mic recognized Landis, and was offended by the comment. Having befriended me many years before, Mic considered me a victim of the movie's terrible accident and legal proceedings. So he had Landis thrown off the aircraft, bags and all.

[Side note: Landis travelled with several production people. They essentially had to deplane with their director, and Captain O'connor left LAX without them.]

The litany of questions was finally over and Mic and I had a hot race to attend. I was fortified with enough story writing and research material to keep me busy for weeks. Lourdes was eavesdropping as she cleaned up around us and I asked my last question. "Mic," I confessed, "You know me, and I know you. But pray tell, where did we first meet?"

The smile returned to Captain O'connor's mustached face. "Oh, that's easy. There was this big forest fire somewhere in Oregon. Evergreen had a few of their helicopters on the fire, called in from many miles away. Sometime after sunset, the crews got showered up and ate dinner, where we encountered our old friends from afar." "You were memorable as you brought with you a rather large leather bag containing an admirable quantity of fragrant 'Thai-Stick.' You were offering some to any of us Veterans who appreciated herbal-stress-management-on-a-stick."

The impenetrable plaque barrier in my cranium that had blocked access to the "O'connor" file for so many years was suddenly flushed aside.

"Oh my!" I wailed. As I rocked back in my chair, Lourdes stopped in her tracks. Her right eyebrow shot up half an inch and stayed there.

In the years before marrying my lovely Latin Lulu', I was rather free-spirited. I could clearly visualize the beloved bag that Mic referred to: my prized stash from The Days of Plenty. Such are the perils of nonfiction.

WILLIAM T. DVORAK

Dustoff Zero-Eight to the Rescue!

Slumped forward in an out-of-place folding chair at the edge of the Santa Clarita River, my mind was reeling from a fiery brush with fate. It was 2:30 in the morning and there was chaos and grim undertakings at hand. My twisted, fire-singed Huey lay on her left side in the current. The "*Twilight Zone, the Movie*" Vietnam village replica was on fire. Slicker-clad firemen rushed onto the flaming set, manning several fire hoses.

A frantic search of the immediate river was underway for three missing actors. Oblivious to the panic, scores of frogs emerged and began croaking in an eerie chorus. A restrained woman wept hysterically. Someone pleaded on a bullhorn, urging everyone to *go home*.

My time in the *Twilight Zone* was just beginning. Accusations would soon start flying, among them *careless and reckless*. I had plenty to worry about. But I also had some *good guys* in my corner - among them William Terrance Dvorak. "Bill" had supervised the rebuilding of the 1960-era UH-1B helicopter that crashed into the river, lying partially burnt and rotors mangled. If anyone came after Western Helicopters, I was confident they wouldn't find anything at fault with N87701, Bill's *Hangar Queen*.

Working with Bill at Western Helicopters for the better part of two years was a rewarding experience for this Vietnam veteran. Bill Dvorak was Western's Director of Maintenance and I served as Director of Operations, and occasional SAG[19] pilot. "Willy T." and I had gone through the same Army helicopter flight school in the late sixties and we both ended up in Vietnam, separated by a year - and one heck of a war story on his behalf.

I never did ask Bill why he signed on to be a "Dustoff" medevac pilot. In fact, I had to dig to discover he was born in a small town in

---

[19] **Screen Actors'** Guild

northeastern Pennsylvania, in 1947. Bill was a self-described *"Pennsylvania-Dutch,"* something he was quite proud of. He studied psychology for two semesters at La Salle College in Philadelphia, Pennsylvania. Bill's mechanical inclinations, apparently, were just coming to the surface.

While he was studying back at LaSalle College in 1966, Bill worked part time at a gas station near the Albert Einstein Medical Center (AEMC) School of Nursing in Philadelphia. Dona Peifer just happened to be studying for her nursing credentials at nearby AEMC.

It turns out that Bill and Dona were dating other friends at the time. His LaSalle College friend Larry Carley suggested that Bill give Dona Peifer a call. They dated for only eight days and love blossomed. [Dona admitted many years later that they "fell hard and fast."]

With the high possibility of being drafted, Bill joined the Army in 1966. After basic training came helicopter flight school. After another ten months of pushups and rigid flight training, Bill then received his Warrant Officer's insignia. The day after - according to tradition - he was awarded his coveted silver wings.

WO1 Dvorak took a fateful step by volunteering to fly air ambulances. To prepare for his deployment to Vietnam, Bill attended Medic Training at Fort Sam Houston, Texas.

In what had to be a very romantic spell, William T. Dvorak proposed to Miss Dona Peifer prior to departing for combat.

Instinct tells me Mr. Dvorak volunteered because *that* was where he felt he could make a difference. And according to the pilots he served with in the 498th Medical Company *Dustoffs*, Bill made a positive difference everywhere he went.

Arriving in Vietnam in August of 1968, Bill was assigned to the 498th at Lane Army Heliport near Qui Nhon, in what was known as *II Corps*, South Vietnam. This brave outfit flew Bell UH-1H air ambulances low-level across the war zone with bright red crosses painted on white backgrounds on the noses and sides of their helicopters, but those green Army Hueys carried no M-60s[20] into battle. That was not their style.

---

[20] One M-60 machine gun per side was the standard armament for all the other Huey's In Country.

Some mighty brave pilots volunteered to fly for the **D**edicated **U**nhesitating **S**ervice **to** **O**ur **F**ighting **F**orces, using their own acronym. Bill Dvorak was in good company.

There were also many brave American nurses working at Tuy Hoa hospital.

Dustoffs' gung-ho, do-or-die attitude originated with legendary Army Major Charles L. Kelly, regarded as the *"Father of Dust Off."*[21] Major Kelly's philosophy concerning a flight to rescue a wounded soldier was: *"No compromise. No rationalization. No hesitation. Fly the mission. Now."* Major Kelly died heroically on the field of battle, living up to his promise. He was awarded the DSC,[22] posthumously.

At the 498th, it was no different. An assignment to *Dustoff* came with the following job description: *Individuals must be willing to fly unarmed helicopters into war zones."To rescue the wounded, under enemy fire."* No sugar coating. Take it or leave it.

Bill's contributions to the 498th included his role as the unit's Aircraft Maintenance Officer, a position that Bill was born to fill. If I've heard him say it once, he's said it a thousand times: "Dorcey, don't you know that *I am the World's Greatest Mechanic?"*

It was a jovial boast, of course, but it told me that Bill had a high opinion of his capabilities in regard to all things mechanical, and helicopters in particular.

The 498th physically resided at Lane Army Airfield. Lane Army Heliport was located in An Son Valley a few miles west-northwest of Qui Nhon, in Binh Dinh Province. Republic of Korea soldiers (ROKs) were in charge of security in the valley, hence the total security at Lane Field. Hueys were kept on the "ready pad" at the ramp, and air crews waited for emergency missions in a "ready room", nearby.

Dustoff Hueys were required to be in the air within two minutes after receiving an urgent call (known as a *Loss of Life is Imminent* mission). After the mission, patients were delivered to the hospital in Qui Nhon, adjacent to the Air Force runway. The *Dustoffs* would then return to Lane Field and prepare for another mission.

---

[21] Originally, *Dustoff* was two words.
[22] The **D**istinguished **S**ervice **C**ross – Second only to the CMOH, the Congressional Medal of Honor.

With several Hueys to wrench on, Bill must have been something of a happy camper to serve as the unit's Maintenance Officer. Of course, he had enlisted mechanics working under him, but he got personally involved and kept the *ambulances* in the air.

Being a warrant officer by job description meant that *flying* was Bill's military *specialty* and flying came *first*. Bill had also signed up for *action* - and as fate would have it - a mere thirty-five days into his tour of duty, Dustoff pilot Dvorak flew into the fire. His crew was sent to evacuate badly wounded soldiers from the 173rd Airborne.

Dustoff 28 pilot, Jim McCollum, also responded to the author's query in the VHPA[23] Aviator, seeking information on Bill's service in Vietnam:

"Bill and I were good friends. We had a million laughs together. I remember the night that he was shot down. It was September 27th, 1968. Bill and I were copilots at the time, and we were both flying missions in support of the 173rd Airborne, who was in heavy contact in an area west of Landing Zone Uplift, and north of Phu Cat Air Force Base."

My A.C. and I were warrant officers. Our aircraft had the hoist in it, so naturally we were hoisting out the wounded that day. We were taking vicious fire from NVA automatic weapons. The 173rd was taking heavy casualties. Toward sunset, Bill's ship flew into LZ Uplift, where we were refueling after dropping off some seriously wounded soldiers.

The 173rd troops in harm's way requested that chain saws and gasoline be lowered down to them, so that they could saw down some trees, making it a little better for the Dustoff aircraft to extract the wounded, although the hoist would still have to be used.

Bill's A.C. out-ranked my A.C. and ordered us to have our crew transfer the hoist to his aircraft. It was an unusual thing to do, but we followed orders.

The troops on the ground were up the side of a steep, heavily forested mountain. The trees were so tall that when you flew over, you were exposed to enemy fire from all over, and it was difficult for the ground troops to direct you, because they could not see through all the smoke and trees.

Bill's A.C. had the saws and gas loaded onto his aircraft. We followed them toward the LZ. As Bill's aircraft arrived over the designated area to lower the chain saws, they received massive automatic weapons fire - as did

---

[23] Vietnam Helicopter Pilots Association

we - hovering just behind them. Our aircraft was hit, and we had warning lights coming on in the cockpit. I saw Bill's aircraft go down simultaneously.

My A.C. made an emergency landing at Phu Cat AFB. On our way to Phu Cat, I made a "Mayday" call for us, and I also reported the downing of Bill's aircraft.

"*Pedro 22*" Air Force Detachment 13, 38th ARRS Crash Rescue, flying a Kaman "Huskie"HH-43B helicopter piloted by Major David H. Pittard and co-pilot Captain Robert N. Bowers launched immediately out of Phu Cat. They headed straight for Bill's last known location in the Suoi Ca Mountains.

Jim continues: *I suggested that they try to get fighter or gunship support before they tried a rescue, but the Pedro flew on. We landed on a taxiway at Phu Cat, and right behind us came Pedro 22, which had been ripped up by forty-eight bullets. The aircraft commander [Major Pittard] was strapped in his seat, mortally wounded.*

Gunships had indeed flown over Bill's crash location trying to draw fire, but the enemy hid, waiting for a less formidable target. The Huskie's other three crewmen were uninjured in the ambush. Major Pittard was DOA at 67th Army Hospital, Qui Nhon.

That evening - Jim concludes - *they finally brought us another helicopter, and we were assigned to fly patients from LZ Uplift and LZ English to the 67th Evac Hospital in Qui Nhon.*

That night, I started smoking cigarettes....

Dustoff 43 pilot Jerry Ewen picks up the story:

"*I was on the scene shortly after Bill's aircraft went down that day, but we could not get to them because of the intensity of enemy automatic weapon fire, and because it was late in the day and darkness fell before the crew could be located.*"

"*The next morning, we had aircraft on station at daylight, and by that time, enemy activity had significantly decreased. We set up an orbit over the area and were looking for our friends. The terrain was hilly, with a major drainage through it that contained small rice paddies. One of our helicopters reported finding and picking up Bill's A.C. and the injured medic.*"

"*It was the worst kind of situation, with our friends on the ground in the midst of the enemy, and we did not know at that point if Bill had survived the shoot-down and the crash.*"

"A few minutes after the A.C. and medic were picked up, we saw another man run out of the tree line into a rice paddy, waving wildly. We immediately dropped down and landed by him, and I saw that it was Bill. He jumped through the open door of the helicopter with the widest grin I think I have ever seen. We were only on the ground for a few seconds, and left as quickly as possible before the enemy had time to get into position. What a relief it was to find him alive and with only minor injuries. He later told us the story about running from the NVA the entire night."

As time would tell, only three of the crew of four in Bill's helicopter survived the crash and overnight ordeal. Sadly, Bill's crew chief – SP4 Ronald L. Granville[24] - died of a broken neck in the crash. The medic suffered a broken leg and had to be assisted by the aircraft commander. Bill broke one of his collarbones and injured both knees, smashing into the instrument panel.

With growing darkness and the determined NVA close enough to hear them, the downed airmen agreed their chances of evading the enemy would be better if they split up. In the rush to avoid being shot or captured, the A.C. took the injured medic with him. Bill set off alone. It would be a long, painful night for the three of them.

Bill's widow, Dona Dvorak, contributed from Tennessee: *(Bill) only talked about being shot down once: he was more likely to mention the absurdity of flying at low altitude with a big red cross painted on the sides of the ship, meaning they were unarmed. The only time he did open up about it, he said how tired and scared he was, running through the rice paddies, falling asleep while moving and waking up face down in the water.*

Bill apparently spent the next six weeks recovering from his injuries In Country. It was during his recovery - Dona informed me - that Bill became interested in becoming a Maintenance Officer. He was eventually examined by a flight surgeon and determined to be healthy enough to return to duty with the 498th.

Dustoff 28 pilot Jim McCollum picks up the story again: "*Two months later – in November of 1968, I flew my first mission as aircraft commander, and Bill was my co-pilot. We had many adventures. Bill was our maintenance officer and did a great job of keeping our aircraft airworthy and available.*"

---

[24] SP4 Granville and Major Pittard's names are engraved on The Vietnam Wall in Washington, D.C.

Jim continues:

"Bill was always bitching at me. He nicknamed me "Lawn Boy," because during several missions – coming out of hot LZs, overloaded with wounded soldiers – I was forced to fly through the trees, chopping them down with the rotor blades. Bill was always asking me, "Do you know how much those blades cost, Lawn Boy?!"

"In February of 1969, my aircraft was shot up. My medic - SP4 Richard J Rochacz - was killed and I was wounded. Bill was talking to me on the radio as I was trying to fly back to the 67th Evac Hospital in Qui Nhon."

When I was lying in the hospital ER - before they wheeled me into surgery - Bill was the first person standing by the gurney - checking on me, and trying to see if the aircraft could be repaired. (It couldn't.)

Bill was also our unit's "scrounger" and could get anything. It was incredible what he could accomplish in that regard.

Although nominated for the Distinguished Flying Cross, Bill declined the honor stating,

"I crashed the helicopter." He wasn't about to take credit for something he didn't "earn."

But following up on his Maintenance Officer ambitions, Bill applied for the AMOC program, to begin once he returned to the USA.

Bill reportedly smoked unfiltered cigarettes throughout his tour of duty, but upon heading home, he dropped the habit. He served exactly one year in the "Vietnam Conflict" and was able to return the USA on August 23rd, 1969 - with a Purple Heart and all kinds of Air Medals to his credit.

Among Bill's air medals was one with "V" for *valor* - and a total of 13 oak leaf clusters - which tells me that Dvorak flew more than his share of dangerous missions as Aircraft Commander *Dustoff Zero Eight*.

With enough "command presence" to satisfy the Army Review Board, and his sights aimed at a career in aircraft maintenance, Bill applied for and was awarded a direct commission, promoting him to First Lieutenant.

Mr. and Mrs. William T. Dvorak were married September 6, 1969, two weeks after Bill's return from the war. Larry Carley – appropriately - served as Bill's Best Man. The Dvoraks later honeymooned at beautiful Fort Eustis, VA.

After the honeymoon, Lt. Dvorak attended the demanding Aircraft Maintenance Officers' Course (AMOC) in Fort Eustis, Virginia. Dona reported that out of the 13 weekends they were in Fort Eustis, it rained on 11 of those weekends.

Following their respective graduations, the Army reassigned Lt. Dvorak to the 206th Aviation Company, in the Republic of Panama. Dona accompanied Bill on his tour of the Canal Zone. Their two young sons, Josh and Travis, were mere twinkles in their eyes at the time. Bill would earn his Captain's bars serving as the unit's Maintenance Director. As fine an officer as he was, the military's Reduction in Force ordered the release of Captain Dvorak from active duty in March of 1975.

With the goal of working in commercial aircraft maintenance and earning his important FAA Airframe & Power-plant license, Bill enrolled at Embry-Riddle in Daytona Beach, FL. Bill also had a couple of flying jobs after leaving the Army, including a job herding cattle on a big Texas spread and maintaining the helicopter on the side.

It was September of 1980 when Bill hired on with Western Helicopters in Rialto, CA. The Dvorak's second son "Josh" was three months old when they moved. Bill and Dona bought a nice place in town near the Country Club, where we became fellow employees and our families became friends.

Dona became a Labor & Delivery or "OB" nurse at a hospital in Riverside. To complicate their lives, they discovered there was *another* Bill Dvorak[25] working at the same hospital, something which would fuel confusion and many jokes over the years ahead.

I had the pleasure of working with several good mechanics while at Western Helicopters, but none were better at the job of Director of Maintenance than Bill. His experience as a captain in the Army had cemented his leadership talents, making him a taskmaster and disciplinarian of the first order.

Pete Gillies - Western's famous Chief Pilot - also admired Mr. Dvorak. When I began working on this story, Pete reminded me of Bill's habit of resting his *"Mickey Mouse ears,"* or hearing-protection-headset clamped humorously on top of his sparsely-haired skull, i.e., after running up a noisy helicopter - leaving them parked thusly for hours.

This amusing practice invited the uninitiated to smirk at his appearance, which usually ended with a snappy rebuke of some kind by the man of many talents. They might as well spite Cyrano's fabled nose!

25

I learned from Bill's *Mickey Mouse* ears that he was not a vain person. He had paid dearly to be in the shape he was in, and there was no covering up his bad knees or the fact that most of his hair had come off inside his flight helmet over the years. This was actually something of a *plus* for his friends, because when one attended the annual Helicopter Association International (HAI) Conventions, flocking to the plethora of Industry lectures that attracted large audiences, one could always locate Bill Dvorak very quickly. What little hair he had stuck straight out on his head and caught the light – just look for the big cocklebur!

Bill's battered knees never stopped bothering him. He limped heavily at times, having to walk around Western's large hangar complex and aircraft parking ramp. Over the years, Dona explained, the Veterans Administration increased his service-connected disability to sixty percent.

Not one to head home at the stroke of five, Bill often worked late along with Pete and me- and other salaried managers, while our wives dealt with our children and prepared the evening meals without us. Our women were as understanding as they could be under the circumstances; their indulgence was never taken for granted.

I remember one night Bill came into Operations to confer with me over something needing my input. Every conversation I ever had with the man was straightforward, and to the point. We didn't waste each other's time with trivia. Jokes, yes! Trivia, no.

I recall Bill sitting in Pete's office chair - his *Mickey Mouse* ears perched on his cocklebur head - thinking about what I had just asked him. When Dvorak was in *high-gear-thinking-mode*, his gaze would shift to an imaginary spot up on the wall behind his observer. Bill would go kind of snake-eyed and softly whistle a curious tune, keeping rhythm with his head while he considered an answer. Whatever we were talking about that evening escapes me, but I clearly recall Bill's young son Travis walking into the room to find his dad. Bill stopped in mid-whistle and was about to ask Travis what he needed, when a familiar, overpowering odor drifted belatedly into the room.

Travis was thought to be "beyond diapers," but he had an *accident*. Bill was very fatherly about it. "I guess we can live with that," he said to his son. The meeting was suddenly over. We were both reminded of what was really important in life; dry pants among them.

Meanwhile, a decade's worth of seismic work in North America had played out, and a mean little recession threatened to put a bunch of helicopter operators in the bread line. The pressure was on management to find other sources of revenue, including taking in outside aircraft maintenance. Bill wasted little time landing paint jobs for his mechanics, and brought in new customers needing complicated stereo installations and medical-evacuation kits.

When the parent company - Rocky Mountain Helicopters - sent us a tired looking (yellow) restricted category UH-1B in need of a complete overhaul, Bill Dvorak had his first California "hangar queen." This was a convoluted project, which would take many months and thousands of dollars in labor to remove over 500 lbs. of unneeded military electrical components and wiring, to lighten up our grand old war bird.

Once N87701 was finally finished, Pete and I had our hands full finding work for the helicopter in an FAA controlled environment, which was not receptive to *restricted category* [read *surplus military*] helicopters. Despite requiring a ton of red tape, several interesting jobs materialized - including setting several power poles for Southern California Edison. There was also an interesting pipeline job on an avocado ranch, and a demanding re-roofing project, all of which proved the versatility of the newly refurbished helicopter.

When our prized Huey was blown out of the sky filming the movie, the impact on Western Helicopters was profound. As if the *Twilight Zone* accident wasn't enough, the commercial helicopter business in 1982 was in dire straits. Dealing with the accident's aftermath took us away from our regular duties and caused us to circle our wagons, as the media was on a feeding frenzy and banging regularly on our door.

In fact, Bill was pictured in *People* magazine and on the front page of *The Los Angeles Times*[26] wearing hip waders while he and investigators from the NTSB combed over the wrecked helicopter, still lying in the Santa Clarita River. From that relationship, the NTSB befriended Bill and had him give a deposition before their first Review Board.

Bill believed me to be the victim of poorly timed special effect explosions, and he displayed that attitude before the Board, gently massaging that possibility into the Investigators' heads. Although I wasn't

---

[26] July 24th edition, 1982.

present, I read the reports and I remember him explaining to the Feds about my attention to detail. "God help anyone who wants an extra hangar key at Western. Dorcey guards the master key roster like a mother bear hovering over her cubs."

Sadly, as indictments were handed down and the accident moved slowly toward the trial stage, Western's parent company began making cuts and selling off assets to keep pace with the dwindling economy. As December rolled around, a company-wide twenty-percent pay cut was announced. I don't think any of us saw it coming; it made us all take a good hard look at our budgets.

As for Bill, it had been a good two and a half years at Western, but he was widely known by then, and guys with his expertise, leadership and piloting ability were in great demand. We tried not to be surprised when he tendered his resignation and went to work for California Helicopters. Our loss, their gain.

Had I been able to, I might have done the same, but my life and career was on hold until the pretrial and trial was over - which would take six long years of litigation. Pete and I continued to grind it out in Operations, flying a mission whenever I wasn't in court, and dealing with one new maintenance chief after another. Man, did we ever miss Bill!

Although both were employed in the outlying cities, Bill and Dona maintained their home in Rialto for several years, enabling the boys to stay enrolled in the local schools and Dona to continue her important hospital career.

It was during this chapter in Bill's life that he became interested in Rialto politics. He served a stint as a City Commissioner, a responsibility I think Bill was destined to love – because of his leadership traits, being a good speaker, and having a genuine fondness to debate the issues.

I missed having Bill's kids in the hangar to help entertain my son Robert. It is hard to explain to one's son that his friends are playing in some distant aircraft hangar now.

I liked how Bill would preflight the company Huey while softly whistling one of his peculiar tunes. He would eventually climb in the left front seat and - in the process of starting up the turbine - he would freeze up if the main-rotor-tie-down wasn't stowed beneath his seat where he could touch it. A man of habit! I wanted to inquire if there was a story behind his paranoia, but I never did.

Another thing Bill did religiously: when he was about to commence work on a helicopter, he always removed his wedding band and placed it neatly in a special green-felt-lined drawer of his tool box. He likewise instructed his mechanics to remove all their rings and bracelets. Pilots and mechanics alike were known to lose fingers - their whole hands, even - while working around the many rapidly rotating components of rotorcraft.

I eventually had the pleasure of employing Bill for his rigging expertise in setting several 4800-lb. "Trane" air-conditioning units on a factory's roof near Camarillo, CA. This was a couple of years after he left Western. When I landed the job, I was unfamiliar with rigging those particular units, but I knew Bill had helped set many of them in place, so I commissioned him to handle the rigging show for me.

When lift day came, I flew the heavy units into place from the left seat of Briles' S-58T helicopter. A lift pilot has his bad days, but not this job. It was reassuring to chat with Mr. Dvorak on the radio, hover over him with several challenging loads; following only his hand signals while blowing dirt everywhere, whipping his "hair" around. It's funny what you remember about a co-worker when he's gone, but those things stand out.

Moving the family east to Tennessee in July of 1996, Bill became the Director of Operations for Aeronautical Accessories, a well-known supplier of crafty after-market helicopter gizmos and safety equipment. In his free time, he turned his political and maintenance expertise into a prestigious position on the Maintenance Technical Committee of the HAI, eventually serving as the Committee's Chairman.

Bill never lost his love for working hands-on with real live helicopters, though - ergo his eventual employment with Air Logistics (Air Log), a major off-shore helicopter operator in the Gulf of Mexico. Bill had a routine work schedule based from the Creole, LA heliport, commuting by air to his Tennessee home on days off.

Helicopters operating off-shore occasionally had problems, and Air Log knew that Bill Dvorak had the right stuff to fly way out to wherever it was on the next available ship, analyze the problem, and get that helicopter back into service. I am sorry to report, it would be Bill's last job.

What happened to my distinguished friend on a fateful day in August, 2005 is really hard to get one's head around. Another pilot with a Flight Instructor and Helicopter Instrument rating perished with Bill that day, the Jet Ranger's assigned pilot. It is not a pretty tale.

Having recently completed Air Log's "new hire" pilot training program, the "Accident Pilot" as we must know him, had slightly less than 2,000 hours total flight time. The pilot's employment records revealed he had 182 hours in the Bell 206. A good start.

The Accident Pilot's problems began after flying over the Gulf of Mexico for an hour and twenty four minutes. It was an uneventful landing at his first stop, dropping off three passengers at their destination. He was preparing to fly to his refueling point - ten minutes away - when he noticed some oil on the helicopter's fuselage. Checking further, no oil was visible in the transmission sight gauge. He did the right thing and called it in. The Accident Pilot was directed to Bill, the troubleshooter on duty.

The Accident Pilot discussed the problem with Bill and a game plan was verbalized over the ship-to-shore radio. He had departed Creole with one hour and fifty minutes worth of fuel, no reserve. Assuming he had enough fuel for a routine post-oil-up ground run and hover test, the Accident Pilot declined an offer (from the pilot who was bringing Bill) to fly him some fuel in portable containers. His response was <u>no</u>; he "..could do this without any problems."

The fates of Bill Dvorak and the Accident Pilot were not sealed at that point. Upon landing at the remote location, Bill determined that the Jet Ranger's transmission had been *over-serviced* - a routine problem with that model, from my own experience.

The oil level was quickly returned to the operating level. Following a five-minute ground-run and a five-minute-hover, everything checked out. By that time, the second helicopter had departed, leaving them to button up and head for some fuel.

Having spent my career as a professional helicopter pilot, I've made my share of mistakes. One thing I *never* did was run out of fuel. Oh sure, I came close a couple of times. But the mere thought of running out of fuel – even when flying alone - scared me into landing short of my destination and making that embarrassing phone call for a fuel truck.

According to tests done afterward on the aircraft's instrument lights, the Accident Pilot ignored the low-fuel light that glows brightly on the instrument panel during the last few minutes of fuel. Also hard to comprehend: the *Emergency Float System* was in the *"unarmed"* position, making a last-second deployment of their inflatable floats unlikely.

Had the Accident Pilot only swallowed his pride - and not blundered inexplicably onward toward the looming rig coming into view over the horizon. As his redemption from poor planning grew closer, the Accident Pilot must have decided anew that there was no need to make a precautionary landing out there on the rolling sea, get shouted at by his boss.

The Accident Pilot apparently believed he was *skillful* enough and *lucky* enough to maintain his altitude and – after using up the very last cup of jet fuel in the tank - shoot an engine-out autorotation to the oil platform's heli-pad. I'll wager that Bill – with no flight controls in front of him – had little choice but watch all of this happen, and hang on. The Accident Pilot was having the worst day of his career and made one bad decision after another; and - from all that can be gleaned from the subsequent federal investigation - ran a perfectly good helicopter out of fuel on short final approach to the rig.

Leaving no room for error, the Accident Pilot's attempt to dodge the platform at the last second resulted in contact between one of the Jet Ranger's two main rotor blades and a steel hand rail, thirty-five feet below the landing deck and seventy-six feet above the water. Oil workers on the rig watched helplessly, eyewitnesses to traumatic destruction.

The noble little helicopter was nearly ripped in two by the impact. The Accident Pilot and The World's Greatest Mechanic were rudely ejected into 190 feet of water. Their bodies were soon recovered, as was most of the wreckage. It was discovered that the pilot had been belted in, but Bill's left-front-seat shoulder harness and lap belt were not fastened. Bill's computer bag and wedding ring were nowhere to be found.

No one I communicate with who knows anything about William T. Dvorak or flying helicopters for a living, has a reassuring moral for me about Bill's premature demise. Oh sure, there's the standard, "He died doing what he loved," and that's appropriate, but I thought about his demise for so long that I literally stopped writing - realizing I couldn't shed any light on what happened, nor lift Bill's story up at the end. I considered dropping everything. *Call it at two books, Wingo* - and write no more.

I sat for hours a day in my humble backyard patio, staring at the cinderblock wall for months on end as I pondered my friend's fate, his unfinished story, and what *Willy T* might have to say about it someday, up there in the Great Beyond. Realizing that was an answer in itself, I contacted Dona Dvorak in Tennessee through a mutual friend, and asked her if we might be able to meet someday and talk about her late husband. In time, we rendezvoused with Dona in Southern California, and together with my wife, had a long conversation in a comfortable old Mexican restaurant near home. I scribbled notes as missing facts and important dates materialized. We found it essential to continue our talk after lunch, resuming the discussion back at our place. It was there Dona told us an amazing story, if not a miracle!

When the Jet Ranger's wreckage was recovered, she disclosed, the aft baggage pod door was open and there was no sign of Bill's black computer bag. Dona knew Bill religiously kept his ring zipped in the bag. She was resigned to the fact that Bill's token of love was in the bottom of the Gulf, lost forever. Two and a half years went slowly by, and then it happened: a blessed shrimp fisherman from San Benito, Texas snagged the bag in his shrimp net! The fisherman located Bill's ID and wedding ring inside, but of course the computer was waterlogged.

The fisherman's nieces back in San Benito were modern gals and Internet users. Through their persistent research, they learned of Bill's accident. Pressing ahead, they were able to track Dona down through her church affiliation. She was listed on her church's web site as the Chairperson of the Finance Committee. *Bingo!*

Dona described the rush of emotion she felt upon learning of this miracle wrapped around a tragedy; at finally being reunited with Bill's ring. It hangs from a gold chain around her neck now, and I wouldn't blame her if she never takes it off.

MAMA CELIA'S CULÍCHE STYLE CHICKEN MÓLE

INGREDIENTS LIST – [FOR SIX HUNGRY PEOPLE]

2 Fresh young chickens - Cut up; fat removed.
1 Bag (8 oz.) dried red chili pods (California or New Mexico grown)
1 Bar unsweetened BAKERS CHOCOLATE
1 Sleeve RITZ CRACKERS, crumbled. (Approx. 36 crackers)
4 TSP Cinnamon
8 Whole Cloves
4 TBS Brown sugar
2 TSP Mazola Oil

Directions ~

- BOIL CHICKEN 30 MINUTES AND SET ASIDE.
- RETAIN TWO CUPS BROTH.
- BOIL THE CHILI PODS UNTIL SOFT, THEN WASH IN COLD WATER.
- REMOVE THE SEEDS & STEMS AND BLEND WITH THE REST OF THE DRY INGREDIENTS.
- IN AN 8 QUART POT, ADD 2 TSP OIL.
- POUR IN THE (STRAINED) BLENDER INGREDIENTS ALONG WITH THE TW0 CUPS OF RETAINED CHICKEN BROTH.
- LET INGREDIENTS BOIL ON LOW FOR ABOUT 30 MINUTES, STIRRING OCCASSIONALY.
- ADD THE CHICKEN TO THE SAUCE AND COOK TOGETHER FOR ABOUT 10 MINUTES, STIR AS NECESSARY.
- SERVE WITH HOT CORN TORTILLAS ON A BED OF MAMA CELIA'S CULÍCHE STYLE SPANISH RICE.
- Enjoy!

GLOSSARY

AAA—Anti-aircraft artillery.

AC—Aircraft, usually helicopters. Also: Aircraft commander, the "command" authority in an aircraft.

A&P—(FAA) Airframe and Power Plant Certification, for mechanics.

AK-47—Standard Warsaw Pact 7.62 x 39MM automatic assault weapon, known for its ruggedness and dependability in the worst conditions. Designed by Mikhail Kalashnikov in the 1940's, it is the most mass-produced assault weapon in the world. It fires at a cyclic rate of around 600 rounds per minute, and a muzzle velocity of 2350 feet-per-second. Also known as the *"AK,"* or *"Kalash."*

AO—Area of operations, terrain.

Army Slick—A troop transport helicopter.

ARVN—Army of the Republic of Vietnam soldiers.

Bell 204B Gunship—[See Bell UH-1C Gunship.]

Bell 205—Civilian version of the UH-1H model Huey.

Bell UH-1C Gunship–A more powerful and maneuverable version of the Bell UH-1B [204B] helicopter. The "C" model employed a new 540 "door hinge" main-rotor, 27-inch cord main-rotor-blades, an improved vertical tail fin, and Lycoming's more powerful T-53-13 turbine engine. Weaponry included twin-flex mini guns and variable-capacity 2.75" folding fin aerial rocket pods, in addition to the two existing crew-manned M60 machine guns.

Birds—Satellites.

Bouncing Betty—Explosive mine that propels up from the ground about four feet into the air and then detonates for more lethal shrapnel effect.

Break Squelch—To send a "click-hiss" signal on a radio by depressing the push-to-talk button without speaking. This brand of radio shorthand was used by LRRPs and others, when actually talking on the microphone might reveal their position.

C-130—Lockheed "Hercules" four-engine, heavy-duty cargo plane.

C-4—A very stable plastic explosive carried by infantry soldiers; bomb and mine component.

CA—Combat assault (troop insertion or extraction), fully coordinated airmobile operation.

CAB—Combat aviation battalion, next higher command over a company.

CAG—Combat aviation group, next higher command over a battalion.

CAV—Nickname for air cavalry, using M113 APCs, and other light armored vehicles.

CCN, CCC, CCS—Command and Control, North (Central or South), the special operations units that ran the clandestine and covert operations in Southeast Asia.

CE—Crew engineer, "crew chief," the helicopter mechanic that kept it in the air, also manned one of the M60 machine guns on a "Slick," or other weaponry on a gunship.

CFI—FAA Certified Flight Instructor.

Chinook—The CH-47, twin rotor, cargo helicopter; also called "Shit hook" or "Hook."

CW2—Chief Warrant Officer, Second Class.

DEROS—Date of estimated return from overseas.

DFC—Distinguished Flying Cross award.

Ergo—So, therefore.

FAA—Federal Aviation Administration; aka *The Friendly Aviators Association*.

FAC—Forward Air Controller, typically an: Air Force Cessna L-19 "Bird Dog;" a centerline-thrust 0-2 Cessna "Skymaster;" or twin-turbine-engine OV-10 "Bronco" spotter plane. The Army also had FACs in the air.

Farnsworth Lantern—A test to determine color blindness by using colored lights.

Fast mover—A jet aircraft, usually an F-4 Phantom.

FBO—Fixed Base Operation. A commercial business located at an active airport. It is regularly open to conduct flights, sell fuel, and/or provide aircraft maintenance.

GHW—Ground handling wheels.

Hobbs Meter—An aviation timer used to record such things as flight time or battery-on time.

Hooch—House, native hut, or GI living quarters.

Horn—Term for radio, or landline telephone. i.e., *Get Sergeant Paradise on the horn, ASAP!"*

HQ—Any headquarters unit, also wherever the CO is located.

Huey—The Bell UH-1 "Iroquois" helicopter, generally configured with an Avco Lycoming turbine engine, with a cruising speed of about 100 knots. Includes UH-1A through M models.

I Corps (pronounced "eye core")—Northernmost military region in South Vietnam beginning around Danang and going to the DMZ, headquarters of I Corps was located in Danang.

II Corps (pronounced "two core")— Area of operations just south of I Corps from south of Danang to south of Cam Ranh Bay.

III Corps (pronounced "three core")— From south of Cam Ranh Bay to north of Saigon.

IV Corps (pronounced "four core")—The southern tip of South Vietnam located in the Mekong River Delta to north of Saigon.

Incoming—Receiving enemy mortar or rocket fire on your position.

INTEL—Intelligence information, also S-2 or G-2.

IP—Instructor pilot, authorized to certify other pilots as flight-ready. Also: CFI

Jolly Green Giant—An Air Force HH-53 heavy rescue helicopter, or also a heavily armed Air Force C-47 aircraft supporting troops.

Juju—Karma.

Klick, "K"—A kilometer, the U.S. military map metric measure equal to 1,000 meters or about 0.6 mile.

Knots—Nautical miles per hour used for stating military aircraft airspeed.

KIA—Killed in action.

Lama—-Aerospatiale's SA-315B model, 5-seat, high-altitude, turbine powered helicopter. It was designed employing an articulated 3-bladed main-rotor and a 3-bladed tail rotor. Its fixed-shaft turbine engine develops approximately 800 SHP.

LOACH—Initially the OH-6A (Hughes) "Cayuse" was used as a "Light Observation Helicopter" (thus the term LOACH), generally single pilot AC employed as aerial scouts to observe the battlefield, direct gunship air coverage and act as an enemy fire 'magnet.' Later during the Vietnam war, the OH-6A was replaced by Bell's "Kiowa," the OH-58. [The commercial version of the Kiowa is known as the Bell 206 "Jet Ranger."]

LRRP— Long range reconnaissance patrol, generally Special Forces Green Berets, and Army Rangers.

LZ—Landing zone—"Hot" LZ is one active with enemy fire.

LZ Prep—Prepare an LZ for landing aircraft and troops by suppressing enemy action through gunship rocket and machine gun fire, artillery bombardment, Air Force fighter jet heavy weapons, and even on rare occasions Navy ship bombardment from offshore.

Lycoming—A large American-based aircraft engine manufacturing company. This company produced the T53-11, and the more powerful T53-13 turbine engines used in most Huey helicopters during the Vietnam Campaign. [A few Air Force UH-1s were powered by GE turbines, installed "backwards."]

M-1—US Army carbine rifle, semi-automatic firing .30 caliber bullet, mostly used in Korea but a few were still found in Vietnam.

M-14—US Army rifle, semi-automatic firing 7.62mm bullet initially used in Vietnam. The military replaced the M-14 with the M-16, except for some forces who retained the M-14 as a sniper rifle.

M-16—US Army rifle, semi-automatic & fully automatic firing a 5.56mm bullet.

M-60—US Army machine gun firing a 7.62mm bullet at approximately 550 rounds per minute.

MPC—Military Payment Certificate, used in lieu of cash or dollars in Vietnam, "funny money."

McDonnell Douglas 500D—The commercial successor to the Hughes 500C, of "Loach" fame. The "D" model utilizes a five-bladed, articulated main-rotor, and a "T" shaped tail fin**.** Performance is further enhanced by either an Allison or a Rolls Royce 420 (SHP) turbine engine, which can propel the streamlined bird up to 156 knots at sea level.

Napalm—Highly flammable explosive used by Air Force fast-movers to burn up an area of suspected enemy activity, or lay down a barrier between friendlies and the enemy.

Nav—Navigational instruments.

NEWBIE—Any person with less time in Vietnam than the person speaking to them.

NVA—North Vietnamese Army soldiers/units

Pendejo—Dummy, literally "pubic hair."

PIC— Pilot in command, different from AC in that PIC was whoever was senior between the two pilots and had not yet received official unit designation as AC.

PP, "Peter Pilot"— An affectionate name for a co-pilot who generally was too inexperienced to be considered of much use other than to change radios, watch AC gauges, and follow the map.

Poncho liner—A light camouflage colored nylon insert to the military rain poncho. It was often used to carry out wounded or deceased soldiers. *Also called a "shelter half."*

Pop Smoke— To mark a team sight location, or LZ, or target with a colored smoke grenade, then a pilot would ID the color to ensure the right location.

Port—Left side.

Repo Depo—A refurb/parts depot/scrapyard for old airplanes and helicopters.

Revetment— The parking place for helicopters.

Roadrunner Team— Team of about 5-6 Green Berets and ARVNs that went in secretly.

ROKs— Republic of Korea soldiers.

RLO—Commissioned Officer, "Real Live Officer."

Sappers—North Vietnamese Army or Viet Cong demolition commandos who infiltrated friendly compounds and planted explosives.

SEA—Southeast Asia, meaning all of that area (not just Vietnam).

SHADOW—AC-119 gunship with 7.62mm and/or 20mm mini guns mounted in side windows.

Snake—The AH-1G Cobra gunship, built specifically as an attack helicopter.

Sniffer Missions—Slicks configured with ammonia sensory devices attached to the skids would fly at low-level above the canopy to detect high levels of ammonia from urine. This often proved to be an indication that enemy troops were in the area, now or recently.

Snoopy Mission—A mission where one helicopter flew at tree-top level, hoping to draw enemy fire. Gunships at a higher elevation would thereby locate the enemy-in-hiding, dive down on them and attack.

Spooky—A C-47 gunship with 7.62 mini guns mounted in the side windows.

Stand-Down— The unit is ordered to rest, re-outfit, and repair for future operations, during which time all operational activity - except for security - is ceased.

Starboard—Right side.

Starlight Scope—A night-vision telescope, used by snipers and basecamp defense troops to see in the dark.

Stick—In a helicopter: the cyclic, which controls fore-aft-and lateral movement; *Slang*: A good pilot.

Stuka—A German made dive bomber.

Tail boom—The aft portion of a conventional helicopter, just behind the engine compartment.

TOC—Tactical Operations Center, pronounced "tock" also called "flight ops" the place in an Avn. Co. where flight missions are generally assigned and posted, a daily and nightly stopping place for crew members.

Transmogrify—Transform grotesquely and humorously.

Twin Otters—De Havilland high-wing twin turbine cargo and passenger aircraft, highly regarded for its maneuverability and ruggedness. Also used as a smoke jumper aircraft by the USFS and the BLM.

USARPAC—United States Army, Pacific Command.

VC—Viet Cong (Vietnamese guerillas).

VFR—Visual Flight Rules. Meteorological conditions which allow a pilot to see and be seen.

www.ingramcontent.com/pod-product-compliance
Lightning Source LLC
Chambersburg PA
CBHW071451070526
44578CB00001B/300